GAME &FISH COOKBOOK

THE GAME
CONSERVANCY
TRUST

GAME &FISH COOKBOOK

THE GAME
CONSERVANCY
TRUST

SWAN·HILL
PRESS

Copyright © The Game Conservancy Trust

First published as in the UK in 1975 by William Collins Ltd
as *The Game Cookery Book* edited by Julia Drysdale

This new edition published in the UK in 2002
by Swan Hill Press, an imprint of Quiller Publishing Ltd
as *Farlows Game & Fish Cookbook*

Reprinted 2004
Reprinted 2006 as *The Game & Fish Cookbook*
with The Game Conservancy Trust

British Library Cataloguing-in-Publication Data
A catalogue record for this book
is available from the British Library

ISBN 1 904057 16 0
     978 1 904057 16 1

Edited by Barbara Thompson

Designed and produced by think : graphic design, Ludlow.

Reprographics by proskanz, Ludlow

Printed in China through Colorcraft Ltd, Hong Kong.

Swan Hill Press
An imprint of Quiller Publishing Ltd
Wykey House, Wykey, Shrewsbury, SY4 1JA
Tel: 01939 261616 Fax: 01939 261606
E-mail: info@quillerbooks.com
Website: www.countrybooksdirect.com

Eaton Hall · Chester

FOREWORD

It is every man's most basic instinct to hunt for and to gather food, to provide for one's self and one's family. The pressures and conveniences of modern life have changed the techniques and methods immeasurably but the motivation remains the same, although often accompanied by increasing concerns over the provenance and quality of the food that we consume.

There has never been a more important time to promote and encourage the consumption of the natural produce of the countryside, unprocessed and untainted by modern production methods. The wild game and fish of our land and shores, which so often have been underutilised in the past, are now increasingly being recognised as the healthiest of all food options. The wider availability in high street superstores and farmer's markets is a most positive development to counter the many diverse threats to the rural economy and the promotion and use of game and fish in everyday cooking is to be both applauded and encouraged.

I am very pleased therefore to be able to commend this new edition of this classic cook book. The sale of each copy will benefit the invaluable work of The Game Conservancy Trust in the preservation of animal habitats and the sustainability of all of our wildlife species and the imaginative and stimulating recipes will further encourage the popularity of game and fish cooking for the benefit of all.

THE DUKE OF WESTMINSTER OBE TD DL

acknowledgements

Recipes

Casserole of pigeon with rice (page 106)
James Beard

Perdrix à la purée de lentilles (page 71)
Faisan à la Cauchoise (page 38)
Pheasant with green peppercorns (page 44)
Faisan au riz Basquais (page 49)
Salsa di lepre (page156)
Venison cutlets in the Ardennes style (page 175)
Cumberland sauce (page 245)
Elizabeth David

Civet of venison (page 170)
Spanish pigeon in chocolate sauce (page 110)
Jane Grigson

Jugged Hare (page 154)
Small Fry Fry-up with Red Pepper Ketchup (page 220)
From: **A Cook on the Wild Side** by Hugh Fearnley-Whittingstall
(Boxtree)

*Saddle of griddled mackerel fillets with sun-dried tomatoes
and fennel seeds*
From: **Rick Stein's Seafood** (BBC Worldwide Ltd)

*Thai trout cakes (page 24, reproduced with the kind
permission of Shooting Times)*
Sweet and sour rabbit (page 138)
Grouse parcels (page 83)
Malted grouse (page 87)
Venison and tomato cobbler (page 177)
Nutty trout (page 215)
Haddrell's trout (page 218)
Angela Humphreys

Mackerel with gooseberries (page 196)
From: **Great British Food** by Heather Hay Ffrench (Quiller Press)

Stir-fried pigeon with chorizo (page 101)
Baked rabbit with red onions, tomato and turmeric (page 139)
From: **Seasonal Bible** by Prue Leith (Bloomsbury). Permission
granted by Peters Fraser & Dunlop on behalf of Leith's School
of Food and Wine.

Pheasant and tarragon creams (page 21)
Spicy salsa smoked salmon pâté (page 15)
Roast aubergines and pheasant breasts with proscuitto (page 36)
Stir-fried pheasant with ginger and apple (page 45)
Pigeon breasts stuffed with cream cheese (page 102)
Stir-fried pigeon (page 111)
Smoked mackerel fishcakes with gherkins (page 197)
Prue Coats

Warm pheasant liver and rocket salad (page 23)
John Robinson, Butchers, Stockbridge

Wine recommendations by H&H Bancroft

Food photography by Michelle Garrett

Home economist: Pippin Britz

Other photographs:
Laurie Campbell 27, 65, 81, 91, 96, 99, 113, 127, 135,
151, 159, 161, 163, 181, 187, 200
Rod Calbrade 15, 23, 41, 50, 125, 225, 270-277
Graham Downing 9, 33, 72, 108
Iain Burn 67

contents

STARTERS

Pâtés & terrines

Any game meat can be used successfully in a pâté or terrine, though if using hare or venison allow rather more fat as their flesh is drier than that of gamebirds.

Some game pâtés have a thin layer of meat running through the middle. In such recipes, strips are cut from the breast and marinated for an hour or more. It is easier to remove the flesh from the bones of a bird if it is partially cooked in a moderate oven (180°C, 350°F, Gas Mark 4) for 20 minutes. Keep all the juices and add them to the pâté.

A good pâté must be given time to ripen and mellow. If time permits, leave the mixture for several hours or overnight before cooking it. After the terrine has cooled, it should be weighted; this gets rid of any pockets of air and makes it firmer and easier to slice.

First cover the top of the pâté with several layers of greaseproof paper, then find a board which fits inside the terrine and stand weights on it. Weights from a traditional set of scales are ideal, though tins from a store cupboard are also effective. The flavour will be further enhanced if it is left for several days in a cool place before eating. How much to serve as a starter is very much a matter of personal choice.

Soup

Game of all types lends itself beautifully to soup. All that is required is a good game stock, made from leftover carcasses, and this will give the base for a variety of excellent soups.

GAME PÂTÉ

350g (12oz)	game meat – liver optional
2 tbs	brandy
1	small onion, minced – optional
25g (1oz)	butter – optional
225g (8oz)	fresh pork fat
8 tbs	wine, port or Madeira
350g (12oz)	lean pork, minced
350g (12oz)	lean veal, minced
1	egg, slightly beaten
½	tsp salt
	generous amount of pepper
6-8	juniper berries, chopped
1	clove garlic, crushed – optional
	thin rashers of streaky bacon to line terrine

Cut some strips 5mm (¼in) thick from the breast of the bird and marinate them in the brandy for an hour or so. Mince the rest of the game with the liver. If using the onion, sauté it slowly in the butter for 5-10 minutes but do not let it brown.

Chop the pork fat into little cubes but retain enough to make strips with, for decorating the top of the pâté. Mix all the ingredients together, including the brandy from the strips of meat but not the strips themselves nor the strips of pork fat. Beat well and allow to rest for at least an hour.

Line a terrine dish with streaky bacon. This is not essential but it helps to keep it together if turning the pâté onto a dish. Place half the mixture in the terrine, then the strips of game and cover with the remaining mixture. Make a criss-cross pattern on the top with the remaining strips of fat. Cover the terrine with foil and then the lid. Set in a pan of hot water in a moderate oven (180°C, 350°F, Gas Mark 4) for about 1½ hours. If the water evaporates, add more. The pâté is cooked when it has shrunk from the sides of the dish.

Cool, then weight until it is cold.

The ingredients can be altered according to personal taste.

NORWEGIAN DUCK TERRINE

For the marinade:

	juice of 1 large orange
2	tbs brandy
1	stock cube, crumbled
1	small onion, finely chopped
	pinch of rosemary

For the pâté:

1	mallard
225g (8oz)	streaky bacon
225g (8oz)	chicken livers
1	Spanish onion, coarsely chopped
1	clove garlic, crushed
50g (2oz)	breadcrumbs

For the garnish:

3 or 4	orange segments
2-3	bay leaves

For the aspic:

12g (½oz)	gelatine (1 sachet)
275ml (½ pint)	less 2 tbs warm stock
2 tbs	orange juice

Combine all the marinade ingredients. Carefully remove 4-5 slices of breast from the duck, then remove all the other flesh and place in the marinade overnight in the refrigerator. Cut the rind from the bacon and flatten each slice with a knife.

Place these around the sides and bottom of a 570ml (1 pint) terrine dish.

Remove the duck from the marinade, mince together all the pâté ingredients, except the strips of breast. Mix into a soft moist paste with the strained marinade and place half the mixture in the terrine, add the strips of breast and cover with the rest of the mixture. Cover and sit the dish in a moderate oven (180°C, 350°F, Gas Mark 4) for 2¼ hours or until a skewer comes out clean. Allow to cool for a few moments and then pour off and retain the juices.

Leave to cool for an hour and then weight the pâté until it is cold. Remove all the fat from the juices. When cold, decorate with orange segments and bay leaves. Warm the orange juice in a pan. Sprinkle over the gelatine and stir until dissolved. Add the stock and strain over the pâté and allow to cool.

PIGEON PÂTÉ

5 or 6	pigeons
2	onions, sliced
2	carrots, sliced
	oil
	flour
450ml (¾ pint)	stock
1 tbs	herbs, chopped
3-5 tbs	red wine, port or brandy
1	clove garlic, crushed in 1tsp salt
	salt and pepper
450g (1lb)	butter
	melted butter

Do not bother to pluck the pigeons, simply skin them, feathers and all, and cut off the breasts. Brown the breasts, onions and carrots in the oil, add a little flour, then the stock, herbs and 2-3 tbs of the wine, port or brandy. Stew slowly until tender – about one hour – and leave overnight.

Next day put the pigeon through a mincer – or a food processor – then add the garlic and work in about 450g (1lb) of softened butter.

Taste and add more seasoning if necessary. If it appears dry, add a little of the liquid in which the pigeons were stewed. Add the remaining red wine, port or brandy. Press into ramekin dishes or a small soufflé dish and cover with melted butter. Allow to set. Serve with hot brown toast and butter.

PHEASANT LIVER PÂTÉ

EASY PÂTÉ

225g (8oz)	pheasant livers
1	tsp salt
	grating of nutmeg
1 tsp	dry mustard powder
⅛ tsp	ground cloves
	small slice onion
	slice of garlic
1-2 tbs	brandy
100g (4oz)	butter, melted

Put the pheasant livers in a pan with just enough water to cover them and simmer for 20 minutes with the lid on. Put them in a liquidizer with all the other ingredients and blend until they have formed a smooth paste. Pour into a shallow dish, cover and chill. If you don't have a liquidizer, mince the cooked livers and then mash them with the rest of the ingredients but have the butter softened instead of melted, chop the onion and mash the garlic.

This can be made using half pheasant livers and half chicken livers.

100g (4oz)	streaky bacon
675g (1½lb)	uncooked or partly cooked game flesh, minced
675g (1½lb)	fat pork, minced
2 tbs	brandy
8 tbs	wine
1	small clove garlic, crushed
1 tsp	salt
	plenty of pepper
6-8	juniper berries, chopped

Chop half the bacon into small squares, reserving the other half, and mix together with the other ingredients. Allow to stand for an hour or so if time permits. Turn into a terrine and decorate with the remaining bacon cut into thin slices and placed diagonally across the terrine. Place, uncovered, in a baking tin of hot water and cook in a slow oven (150°C, 300°F, Gas Mark 2) for 1¼ to 1½ hours. The pâté is cooked when it starts to come away from the side of the dish. Allow to cool and then weight it.

POTTED GAME

225g (8oz)	cooked game meat, without skin or sinews
50g (2oz)	cooked ham, with plenty of fat
65g (2½oz)	clarified butter
	salt and pepper to taste
	a little cayenne pepper
	few drops of lemon juice
	melted butter for sealing (preferably clarified)

Chop the meat coarsely (do not mince it) and add the clarified butter. This is better pounded with a pestle and mortar, but if time is short it can go in the liquidizer.

Season generously and add the cayenne pepper and lemon juice. Pack it into small china or glass pots and when these are cold, cover with warm, but not hot, clarified butter.

If using older game which has been stewed first, make sure it is absolutely dry otherwise the moisture will collect at the bottom of the pots. Well stewed venison in red wine and seasoning is usually more successful than roast venison.

POTTED SALMON

This does not keep as well as potted meat and should be eaten fairly quickly

Use equal quantities of:

cooked, boned and skinned salmon and softened butter

a little white pepper

a little white wine or lemon juice

a pinch of nutmeg

melted clarified butter

Pound all the ingredients well together. Add only enough wine or lemon juice to make the consistency soft and even.

Test for seasoning, put into small pots and leave to cool.

When cold, cover with a layer of warm, but not hot, clarified butter.

SPICY SALSA SMOKED SALMON PÂTÉ

Prue Coats

225g (8oz)	smoked salmon
100g (4oz)	softened butter
	lemon juice to taste
1 tbs	chopped coriander or parsley
1 pinch	dried marjoram
1 tsp	coriander seeds
½tsp	finely chopped green chilli
½tsp	finely chopped red chilli
	salt and pepper

Place the salmon, butter and lemon juice in a food processor and blend until smooth. Crush the coriander seeds in a pestle and mortar then add these, with the rest of the ingredients, to the salmon mixture (add chilli a little at time, according to taste). Spoon into a dish and refrigerate for at least 24 hours. Take out 2 hours before serving. Serve with taco corn chips.

Serves 4-6

SMOKED FISH TERRINE

350g (12oz)	smoked salmon or trout, sliced
100-150g (4-5oz)	smoked salmon pâté,
	home-made or bought
100-150g (4-5oz)	smoked trout pâté,
	home-made or bought
100-150g (4-5oz)	smoked mackerel pâté,
	home-made or bought
100-175g (4-6oz)	cooked spinach or asparagus
	(if in season)
1 tsp	tomato purée
1-2 tsp	horseradish (according to taste)
	bed of salad leaves

Line a 1lb bread tin with cling film (leaving enough on each side to fold over the top) and grease it lightly with oil. Line the base and sides of the tin with the slices of smoked salmon or trout – again allowing enough to fold over the top. Spoon in the smoked trout pâté and spread out to make an even layer; add a thin layer of cooked spinach or asparagus. Combine the smoked salmon pâté with the tomato purée and spread on top of the spinach or asparagus. Add another thin layer of spinach or asparagus, then mix the smoked mackerel pâté with the horseradish to make the final layer of the terrine. Fold the smoked salmon over, pull the cling film over the top and refrigerate overnight.

The following day, turn out the terrine, cut into slices and serve on a bed of salad leaves.

Serves 6

GAME SOUP

This may vary enormously depending on what meat, bones or carcass of game are available.

For the stock:

1 tbs	pork or bacon dripping, or butter
1	onion, sliced
1	leek, cut in 2.5 cm (1in) pieces
3	carrots, sliced
1	stalk celery, sliced
450g (1lb)	stewing venison, diced
1-2	carcasses (gamebird or chicken)
1	pig's trotter
1	knuckle of veal (optional)
6	parsley stalks
6	peppercorns
4	juniper berries
1	bay leaf
	a pinch of thyme
	beurre manié
	salt and pepper
	port, lemon juice or redcurrant jelly (optional)

Melt the fat in a large pan, stir in the vegetables and cook lightly. Add the venison, carcasses, pig's trotter and veal (if using) and brown slightly, then add the herbs and 1¾ litres (3 pints) cold water. Bring to the boil and simmer for about 3 hours. Skim and strain.

Having made the game stock, reserve a few pieces of meat, throw away the bones and any skin and liquidize the remaining meat and vegetables. Return to the stock and thicken with a little beurre manié (1 tbs butter mixed with 1 tbs flour) adding a little at a time, whisking well. Season with salt and pepper and add some port, lemon juice or redcurrant jelly – the latter would suit a venison soup rather than one made with feathered game. Add the pieces of meat, and heat the soup until it is very hot.

For a creamy soup, beat 3 egg yolks into 275ml (½pint) cream or crème fraîche. Beat this mixture into a cup of hot game stock and then incorporate into the remaining stock. Continue to beat over a low heat until the soup has thickened, but do not let it boil.

Serves 6

GAME CONSOMMÉ

game stock (see page 17)

sherry, port or Madeira to taste

a little rice or small pasta shapes, cooked

3-4 mushrooms finely sliced,

sautéed in butter – optional

Prepare the stock as for the game soup. When cold, skim off the fat and add sherry, port or Madeira to taste. Fold in the rice or pasta and the finely sliced mushrooms, if using.

Serves 6

GAME AND LENTIL SOUP

1.2-1.75 litres	good game stock
(2-3 pints)	
350g (12oz)	mixed lentils
2	onions, chopped
2	carrots, peeled and chopped
2–3	celery stalks, chopped
2	cloves garlic, crushed
450g (1lb)	potatoes, peeled and cut
	into 2cm (¾in) dice
100g (4oz)	lardons, streaky bacon or ham
2 tbs	fresh parsley, chopped
1 tsp	mixed dried herbs
	salt and pepper
	pieces of meat from the carcass – optional

Place all the ingredients in a large saucepan and bring to the boil. Simmer, half covered, for about an hour until the lentils are soft. Serve with lots of crusty bread.

For a smoother consistency blend the soup in a liquidizer.

Serves 6

PARTRIDGE AND CABBAGE SOUP

This is almost a meal in itself.

2	old partridges, skinned but not plucked, cut into pieces
100g (4oz)	lean smoked bacon or ham, or a smoked pig's trotter
3 litres (6 pints)	water
900g (2lb)	cabbage, sliced thickly
8–10	peppercorns, crushed
2	cloves garlic, crushed
2	medium onions, sliced
2	carrots, sliced
1	bouquet garni (consisting of 6 sprigs parsley, one bay leaf)

Put the partridges, bacon and water in a large pot and bring to the boil. Add all the other ingredients. Bring back to the boil, cover and simmer for 2–3 hours or until the partridges are tender. Strain and discard the bones, skin, parsley and bay leaf. Remove the bacon and partridges. Cut the meat into small pieces and return to the soup.

If desired, the soup can be blended in a liquidizer and thinned down with stock or single cream.

Serves 6–8

SALMON SOUP

1	salmon head and bones
450g (1lb)	raw fish bones and trimmings
	(available from most fishmongers)
1	leek, chopped
1	stalk celery, chopped
1	large onion, chopped
1	clove garlic
2 tsp	salt
12	peppercorns
1	bay leaf
	bunch of parsley with stalks
1½ litres (2½pints)	water
2 tbs	olive oil
1	onion, chopped
3	white parts of leeks, chopped
3	large tomatoes, skinned and chopped
275ml (½pint)	white wine
	salt & pepper
4 tbs	double cream or
	crème fraîche (optional)

This is an excellent way of using up the carcass of a salmon. If possible, reserve some of the flesh to put in the soup.

Place the first 11 ingredients in a large saucepan and boil for about 30 minutes. Strain. Heat the olive oil in a saucepan and lightly fry the onion and leeks. Add the tomatoes, fish stock and wine. Cook for 20 minutes. Test for salt and pepper and add the cream or créme fraîche, if using.

Just before serving, add any leftover flakes of salmon.

Serves 6

A small tin of salmon may be added to the soup.

SMOKED FISH CHOWDER

25–50g (1–2oz)	butter
1	onion, finely chopped
2–3 tbs	flour
450ml (¾pint)	hot milk
450ml (¾pint)	fish stock
	salt and pepper
225–350g (8–12oz)	smoked fish – eg trout
450g (1lb)	potatoes, peeled and diced
	small can sweetcorn – optional

Melt the butter in a frying–pan and gently fry the onion until soft but not brown. Stir in the flour and cook for 2 minutes, stirring. Gradually stir in the hot milk and stock and slowly bring to the boil. Season and add the potatoes. Cover and simmer for about 20 minutes until the potatoes are soft. Cut the trout into chunks and fold into the chowder with the sweetcorn, if using.

Serves 4–6

PHEASANT & TARRAGON CREAMS
Prue Coats

225g (8oz)	cooked pheasant meat
2 tbs	good quality mayonnaise
4 tbs	Greek yoghurt
12g (½oz)	gelatine (1 sachet)
1 tbs	fresh tarragon, chopped
	water or stock
	tarragon vinegar or lemon juice
	salt and pepper

Put the meat in a blender or liquidizer with the mayonnaise and yoghurt and blend until it is creamy. Spoon into a measuring jug.

Prepare the gelatine according to the packet, add to the mixture in the jug and make up the quantity to 570ml (1 pint) with cold stock or water.

Stir in the tarragon, add a little vinegar or lemon juice and season to taste. Oil six ramekins and fill with the mixture.

Turn out when set, and garnish to taste.

Serves 6

Chopped fennel can be used instead of tarragon.

WARM GAME SALAD

For the dressing:

4 tbs	olive oil
1 tbs	balsamic vinegar
	a pinch of sugar
½	clove garlic, crushed
	salt and pepper

25–50g (1–2oz)	butter
100g (4oz)	lardons
100g (4oz)	chestnut mushrooms, sliced
225g (8oz)	cold cooked game, such as pheasant, partridge or grouse
2–3	spring onions, cut into 2.5cm (1in) strips
	salad leaves

First make the dressing by whisking together the oil, balsamic vinegar and garlic. Mix thoroughly and add sugar, salt and pepper to taste.

For the salad: melt the butter in a large frying–pan and gently fry the lardons until golden; stir in the mushrooms and fry for another 2 minutes. Cut the game into thin strips and toss into the frying–pan with the spring onions, until warmed through. Serve on a bed of salad leaves with the dressing drizzled over.

Serves 4

WARM PHEASANT LIVER & ROCKET SALAD

25g (1oz)	butter
4	pheasant livers, sliced
1	clove garlic, crushed
	a little rosemary, chopped
	a squeeze of lemon juice
	salt and pepper
	fresh rocket

Melt the butter in a frying–pan and sauté the pheasant livers with the garlic and rosemary for 2–3 minutes. Add a little lemon juice, season to taste and arrange on a bed of rocket.

Serves 2

This works well with chicken livers or a combination of pheasant and chicken livers.

THAI TROUT CAKES
Angela Humphreys

450g (1lb)	trout, boned and cut into chunks
1	egg beaten
1	small red chilli, deseeded
2 tsp	Thai red curry paste
	juice of ½ lime
1 tsp	brown sugar
1 tbs	chopped coriander
	salt
½	green pepper, very finely chopped
½	red pepper, very finely chopped
	oil for frying

For the sauce:

3 tbs	Thai fish sauce
2 tsp	white wine vinegar
	juice of ½ lime
1 tsp	brown sugar

Place all the fish cake ingredients, except for the chopped pepper and oil, in a bowl and mix thoroughly or chop in a food processor for 30 seconds.

Add the chopped peppers and mix well.

Carefully shape the mixture into small cakes. Deep fry in oil for 5 minutes or until they are golden brown.

Combine all the sauce ingredients and serve separately. Garnish the fish cakes with lime wedges.

Serves 4–6

PHEASANT

The pheasant is by far the most plentiful of Britain's game species and, indeed, the best known. Oven-ready pheasants can be bought from game dealers, butchers or supermarkets and are available fresh from October to February, or frozen when out of season.

Freshly shot birds may be hung by the neck in a cool, well-ventilated, fly-proof place for anything up to 10 days, depending on the weather conditions. The hanging process heightens the "gamey" flavour of the bird and how long to hang is a matter of personal taste. Older birds are generally hung for longer than younger ones as this helps to tenderize the meat.

When the bird has been hung for the desired amount of time, it must be plucked, drawn and, if it is being cooked whole rather than in pieces, trussed. For more information about preparing game, see page 270.

Almost any robust chicken recipe will adapt to pheasant. Young pheasants are delicious roasted, but if there is any doubt as to the age of the bird, assume it to be a mature one and cook it accordingly as a pot-roast or a casserole. All the recipes are for oven-ready pheasants.

For details of how to joint a pheasant or to take off the breasts only, see page 272.

One pheasant will serve two to four people, depending on its size, and can be served slightly pink.

Wine recommendation

Pheasant is perfectly suited to Burgundy Pinot Noir, however, the older the bird and the stronger the flavours, the more you can experiment. Plain roasts love a good Vosne-Romanée; braised pheasant is excellent with reds from southern France or new world Shiraz. Anything with spirits in the recipe will be complemented by a young Bordeaux. In the cold January months a spicy or ginger flavoured pheasant is delicious with a northern Rhône such as Hermitage or Côte-Rôtie.

ROAST PHEASANT

1   young pheasant

1   apple, cored and chopped

½   onion, chopped

2 tbs   butter

      salt and freshly-ground black pepper

3   slices streaky bacon or pork fat

For the stock:

      giblets from the pheasant

1   slice onion

2-3   slices carrot

1   bay leaf

      a little port (optional)

Place the apple and onion inside the bird, together with 1 tbs of the butter, three or four good turns of the pepper-grinder and a little salt. Ensure the bird is well-trussed and rub it all over with the remaining butter.

Cover the breast with streaky bacon or pork fat and place in a preheated oven, (180°C, 350°F, Gas Mark 4), breast-side down, for about 1 hour (depending on the size of the bird) basting as often as possible. Remove the bacon or fat for the last 10 minutes and turn the bird the right way up to allow the breast to brown. The pheasant is cooked when the juices run clear. Allow the pheasant to rest, in a warm place, for at least 20 minutes before serving.

While the pheasant is cooking, put the giblets in a pan of water, together with a slice of onion, 2-3 slices of carrot and a bay leaf, bring to the boil and simmer for about an hour.

Make a thin gravy mixing the juices from the roasting pan with the strained stock and a little port, if using. Season to taste. Roast pheasant is traditionally served with game chips, fried breadcrumbs and/or bread sauce, (see pages 255, 264, 238).

Serves 2-4

If using a roasting pan with lid, the pheasant will take a little longer, about 1¼ hours. There is no need to baste.

MARINATED PHEASANT

PHEASANT IN A CHICKEN BRICK

4 pheasant breasts

   drizzle of olive oil

For the marinade:

2 tbs soy sauce

2 tbs clear honey

1-2 tbs Tabasco green pepper sauce

2 large cloves garlic, crushed

2.5cm (1in) piece fresh ginger, grated

   juice of ½ lemon

Mix all the marinade ingredients together in a bowl. Place the pheasant breasts in the mixture, cover with cling film and marinate for at least an hour.

Remove the breasts and place each on a large sheet of foil. Pour a little of the marinade onto each breast, drizzle over a little olive oil and wrap tightly into a parcel.

Cook in a moderately hot oven (190°C, 375°F, Gas Mark 5) for 35-45 minutes.

Serves 4

A chicken brick (obtainable from most good kitchen shops) helps keep the meat moist.

2 small pheasants

2 tbs olive oil (preferably herb-flavoured)

4-5 juniper berries

   salt and pepper

2 slices streaky bacon

Rub the pheasants all over with the olive oil (any herb-flavoured olive oil works well or plain will do). Place the juniper berries inside the birds with the salt and pepper. Season the outside as well, place the bacon over the breast and put in the brick. Place the brick in a cold oven, set very hot (230°C, 450°F, Gas Mark 8), and bake for 1½ hours. A few vegetables, such as onions, carrots or celery, may be placed under the birds.

Serves 2-4

Other excellent ways of keeping pheasant meat moist include cooking in a metal roasting pan with a lid or a roasting bag. Both methods will require a cooler, preheated oven; follow the manufacturer's guidance.

PHEASANT BREASTS WITH SUN-DRIED TOMATOES

2	pheasant breasts
2	rashers of smoked streaky bacon

For the stuffing:

2oz	brown breadcrumbs
1oz	chopped sun-dried tomatoes
1	clove garlic, crushed
	a few fresh basil leaves, chopped or torn
	a few drops of olive oil

Combine the stuffing ingredients and stir well. With a sharp knife, cut a pocket in each breast and push in the stuffing as evenly as possible.

Wrap a rasher of bacon round each breast and secure with toothpicks. Place in an oven-proof dish, cover with buttered paper or foil and cook at a moderately hot temperature (190°C, 375°F, Gas Mark 5) for 35-45 minutes, removing the paper or foil for the last 15 minutes.

Serves 2

PHEASANT IN SOUR CREAM

1	young pheasant, cut into quarters
2 tbs	olive oil
2 tbs	butter
	seasoned flour
570ml (1 pint)	sour cream or crème fraîche
1 tbs	paprika
2 tbs	chopped parsley

Heat the oil and butter in a heavy casserole. Dredge the pheasant pieces in seasoned flour and cook them carefully in the fat so that they remain just golden. Pour over the sour cream, paprika and parsley, bring to a simmer, cover the casserole and cook gently for about 45 minutes.

Serve with boiled new potatoes added to the dish just before serving, or with noodles.

Serves 2-4

BRAISED PHEASANT

1	pheasant
2 tbs	butter
2	carrots, sliced
1	onion, sliced
4	sticks of celery, chopped
4	sprigs of parsley, chopped
	salt and pepper
150ml (¼pt)	game stock
275ml (½pt)	red wine
2 tbs	good quality redcurrant jelly

Melt the butter in a large frying-pan and brown the pheasant all over. Make a bed of the vegetables in the bottom of the casserole and place the pheasant on top, together with some salt and pepper. Pour over the stock and red wine, cover, and cook in a moderate oven (180°C, 350°F, Gas Mark 4) for about 1 hour, basting occasionally. Remove the casserole from the oven, strain off the gravy and thicken, if necessary, with a little cornflour. Add the redcurrant jelly, simmer until the jelly has dissolved and pour back over the bird. The vegetables can be left as they are or liquidized and incorporated into the gravy.

Serves 2-4

CASSEROLED PHEASANT WITH CHESTNUTS

1	pheasant
25g (1oz)	butter or 1 tbs oil
350g (12oz)	chestnuts, peeled
	(fresh, tinned or vacuum-packed)
225g (8oz)	button onions or shallots
25g (1oz)	flour
570ml (1 pint)	good stock
	grated rind and juice of 1 small orange
2 tsp	good quality redcurrant jelly
100ml (4fl oz)	red wine
	bouquet garni
	salt and pepper
2 tbs	chopped parsley

Melt the butter or oil in a large frying-pan and brown the pheasant all over. Remove from the pan. Sauté the onions and chestnuts briskly until they begin to turn brown, shaking the pan frequently. Remove from the pan and add enough flour to take up the remaining fat. Mix well, add all the remaining ingredients, except the parsley, and bring to the boil.

Place the pheasant in a casserole, surround with chestnuts* and onions, pour over the sauce and cover tightly.

Cook in a moderately slow oven (160°C, 325°F, Gas Mark 3) for 1-1½ hours.

Remove the bird and cut into joints; place in a deep serving dish with the chestnuts and onions. Remove the bouquet garni, skim the fat from the liquid, season to taste and pour over the pheasant. Sprinkle with parsley.

*If using pre-cooked chestnuts, add to the casserole for the final half hour only.

Serves 2-4

PHEASANT IN RED WINE

2	pheasants, jointed
3 tbs	butter
2 tbs	oil
100g (4oz)	lardons (bacon cut into small cubes)
15-20	button onions or shallots
1	clove garlic, crushed
50ml (2fl oz)	brandy
¾ bottle	good red wine
275ml (½ pt)	game stock
½ tbs	tomato purée
	salt and pepper
	bouquet garni
225g (8oz)	mushrooms
	beurre manié (3 tbs flour worked into 2 tbs softened butter)
To serve:	croutons fried in butter

Melt 2 tbs of the butter and the oil in a heavy casserole and brown the lardons, onion and garlic lightly. Remove with a slotted spoon and brown the pheasant pieces, a few at a time, adding more fat if necessary. Put all the pheasant pieces back into the casserole, cover and heat for a few minutes, then pour over the brandy and ignite.

Return the lardons, onion and garlic to the casserole, pour over the wine and strained stock to cover the pheasant. Stir in the tomato purée, season with salt and pepper, and add the bouquet garni. Cook in a preheated oven (180°C, 350°F, Gas Mark 4) for 20 minutes, then reduce the temperature to (160°C, 325°F, Gas Mark 3) and cook for another ¾-1 hour, until the pheasant is tender.

Return the casserole to the hob, discard the bouquet garni and add the beurre manié in small pieces, stirring all the time, and simmer until the sauce thickens. Sauté the mushrooms in the remaining butter for about a minute and add to the casserole. Serve with croutons.

Serves 4-6

Lardons are available from good supermarkets.

ROAST AUBERGINES AND PHEASANT BREASTS WITH PROSCIUTTO
Prue Coats

4	pheasant breasts
	oil
4	slivers of feta cheese
4	slices of prosciutto or Parma ham
2	aubergines
1-2 tbs	tomato ketchup
	dash of Worcester sauce
	dash of soy sauce
	dash of Tabasco
2 tsp	italian mixed herbs
2-3 tbs	olive oil

Cut slits lengthways in the breasts and insert the slivers of feta cheese. Smear the breasts with oil and wrap in the prosciutto, securing with toothpicks if necessary. Cut the aubergines into 5cm (2in) chunks and put in a bowl. Add the tomato ketchup, Worcester sauce, soy sauce, Tabasco and herbs to taste and stir in the olive oil. Mix well.

Spread the aubergine mixture onto an oven tray and place in a moderately hot oven (200°C, 400°F, Gas Mark 6) for 25 minutes, then add the pheasant breasts and cook for a further 20 minutes. Stir the aubergine mixture and turn the pheasants halfway through the cooking time.

Serve with pasta.

Serves 2-4

This can also be eaten cold.

DUNTREATH PHEASANT

1	pheasant, jointed
100g (4oz)	butter
2	large onions, chopped
1	green pepper
1	large stick of celery, chopped
275ml (½pt)	white wine
Pinch each of	mixed herbs, cinnamon, thyme, nutmeg, cloves
275ml (½pt)	double cream or crème fraîche

Fry the pheasant in the butter for 10 minutes, turning frequently. Remove and keep warm, then add the onions and green pepper and celery. Fry gently then add the wine and seasonings and bring to the boil.

Remove from the heat, stir in the cream or crème fraîche, return the pheasant pieces to the pan and heat very gently for 30 minutes.

Serves 2-4

If the sauce looks a little curdled, beat in more cream off the heat; this should give a smoother texture.

FAISAN AUX NOIX

4	pheasant breasts, skinned
4	strips bacon
1 tbs	olive oil and 1 tbs butter for frying
12	pickled walnuts, quartered
	juice of 1-2 oranges
5 tbs	Madeira
	salt and pepper
5 tbs	stock

Wrap the pheasant breasts with the bacon strips and secure with toothpicks. Melt the butter and oil in a heavy casserole and brown the pheasant breasts, then add the walnuts, orange juice, Madeira, salt and pepper. Cook for 45 minutes over a medium heat, until cooked through. Add stock and allow to simmer for a few minutes. Serve the sauce separately.

Serves 4

FAISAN À LA CAUCHOISE
(PHEASANT WITH CREAM, CALVADOS AND APPLE)
Elizabeth David

1	**young pheasant**
small glass	**Calvados (or brandy or whisky)**
250-275ml (8-10fl oz)	**double cream or crème fraîche**
	salt and pepper
2	**dessert apples**
1 tbs	**butter**

Brown the pheasant in the melted butter in a heavy iron or earthenware pot on top of the oven, turning it over once or twice so that each side is nicely browned. Transfer to a moderate oven (180°C, 350°F, Gas Mark 4) and cook for about 1 hour*. Remove, allow to rest, and carve into slices. Transfer the meat to a serving dish and keep warm.

Pour off the juices from the meat into a shallow pan, and heat, allowing them to bubble; pour in a small glass of warmed Calvados (or brandy or whisky), set light to it, shake the pan, and when the flames have burnt out add the double cream or crème fraîche. Shake the pan, lifting and stirring the cream or crème fraîche until it thickens. Season with a very little salt and pepper. Pour the sauce over the pheasant.

Serve separately a little dish of diced sweet apple, previously fried golden in butter and kept warm in the oven.

Alternatively the pheasant can be cooked on the hob for about 45 minutes.

Serves 2-4

SPICY PHEASANT

1	young pheasant
2 tbs	seasoned flour
2 tbs	butter
2 tbs	oil
For the sauce:	
3-4 tbs	honey
3-4 tbs	redcurrant jelly
3 tbs	tomato ketchup
1 tbs	tomato purée
2-3 tbs	soy sauce
3 tbs	red wine vinegar
450ml (¾ pint)	stock

Cut the pheasant into 2-4 pieces, depending on size, and dip the pieces in the seasoned flour. Melt the butter and oil in a heavy frying-pan and brown the pheasant quickly all over. Lower the heat, cover, and cook slowly until tender and the juices run clear, about 25 minutes.

To make the sauce, combine all the ingredients in a saucepan, bring to the boil, stirring all the time, until reduced to a thick syrup. Season to taste.

Serve the pheasant pieces on a warm platter with the sauce poured over.

Serves 2-4

INDIAN PHEASANT

2	pheasants
4 tbs	ghee or butter
2 tsp	ground coriander
½ tsp	ground chillies
1½ tsp	ground cumin
1 tsp	ground cardamon
½ tsp	ground turmeric
½ tsp	ground pepper
1 tsp	salt
½ tsp	mixed spice
1	large onion
1	clove garlic, mashed
2	crisp apples, peeled and diced
570ml (1 pint)	stock
1	bay leaf
4cm (1½in)	cinnamon stick
	juice of ½ lemon
2 tsp	redcurrant jelly
275ml (½ pint)	coconut milk

The flavour is improved if the spices are ground at home in a food processor or pestle and mortar.

Roast the pheasants in a moderate oven (180°C, 350°F, Gas Mark 4) for approximately 20 minutes. Remove from the oven and, when cool, start taking the meat off the carcass and cut into bite-size pieces (the bones and remaining meat can be used for stock).

Heat the ghee or butter in a large frying-pan. Add all the dried spices and fry gently for a few minutes. Add the onion, garlic and apple, and fry until soft. Add the pheasant chunks, and keep turning until well coated and brown. Add the stock, bay leaf, cinnamon stick, lemon juice and redcurrant jelly. Simmer over a low heat for 1-1½ hours until the meat is tender.

Add the coconut milk for the last 10 minutes and thicken if necessary with a little cornflour mixed with water.

Serve with sweet mango chutney and cucumber raita (see opposite).

Serves 4-6

Ghee is available from most good supermarkets.

CUCUMBER RAITA

1	large cucumber
	salt
125ml (¼ pt)	plain, fat-free yoghurt
	black pepper
	sugar to taste

Peel the cucumber and grate coarsely onto a plate. Sprinkle with salt, cover and stand the plate in the refrigerator or in a cold place for 30 minutes. Drain the cucumber thoroughly. Mix it with the yoghurt in a bowl and add black pepper and a little sugar to taste.

CORONATION PHEASANT

An adaptation of Coronation Chicken, created for HM The Queen's coronation in 1953. The curry mixture makes double that required for one pheasant, so half can be frozen and kept for another occasion.

1.6-1.8kg(3-4lb)	pheasant (either one large pheasant or two smaller ones)
	slices of carrot and onion,
	a bay leaf and peppercorns
	salt and pepper
225g (8oz)	onion, chopped
50g (2oz)	butter
8	no-soak dried apricots
	grated rind of 2 lemons
4 tbs	runny honey
5 tbs	medium curry paste
450ml (¾ pt)	dry white wine
4-5 tbs	(or to taste) good quality mayonnaise
3 tbs	double cream

Place the pheasant in a large saucepan and cover with water to the top of the pan; add the carrot, onion, bay leaf and peppercorns with a large pinch of salt. Bring to the boil, cover and simmer until the pheasant is thoroughly cooked – about an hour. Leave to cool in the liquid.

Cut the pheasant into bite-sized pieces, discarding the skin and bone.

Sauté the chopped onion in the melted butter until softened. Add the apricots, grated lemon rind, honey, curry paste and white wine. Simmer, uncovered, for 30-40 minutes or until the curry mixture is the consistency of thin chutney. Cool. Blend in a food processor or liquidizer, then sieve if necessary. Stir half the curry mixture into the mayonnaise (freeze the remainder). Mix in the double cream and season to taste.

Fold the pheasant through the sauce (this can be done the day before, then covered and refrigerated). Serve on a bed of rice salad and garnish with fresh herbs.

Serves 4 as a main meal or 6 as part of a buffet.

Boned pheasant breasts can be used instead – just poach in boiling water or stock for about 15-20 minutes.

GOLDEN JUBILEE PHEASANT

A variation of Golden Jubilee Chicken, created by Lionel Mann to mark HM The Queen's Golden Jubilee in 2002.

4	pheasant breasts
	salt and pepper
	grated nutmeg
2 tbs	olive oil
1	bunch flat leaf parsley
1	lime, quartered

For the marinade:

	juice and zest of ½ lime
2.5cm (1in)	fresh root ginger, peeled and grated
1	clove garlic, crushed
1	shallot, finely chopped
2 tbs	olive oil

For the dressing:

100ml (4fl oz)	crème fraîche
6 tbs	good quality mayonnaise
	juice and zest of ½ lime
5cm (2in)	piece fresh ginger

Mix all the marinade ingredients together in a shallow dish. Add the pheasant and turn to coat thoroughly. Cover and refrigerate for 2-3 hours.

For the dressing, mix the crème fraîche, mayonnaise, lime juice and zest in a bowl. Peel and grate the ginger and either twist in a piece of muslin or press through a sieve to extract the juice. Add 2 tsp of the ginger juice to the dressing. Stir, cover and chill.

Scrape the marinade from the pheasant breasts and pat dry with kitchen paper. Season with salt, pepper and freshly grated nutmeg and place in a roasting tin. Drizzle over the olive oil. Roast in a moderately hot preheated oven (190°C, 375°F, Gas Mark 5), basting occasionally, for 20-25 minutes until the pheasant is cooked through.

Leave the pheasant to cool completely, then cut into bite-sized pieces. Combine the pheasant and dressing, adjust the seasoning and refrigerate until needed. Serve with pasta salad, lime quarters and chopped flat leaf parsley.

Serves 4

PHEASANT WITH GREEN PEPPERCORNS

Elizabeth David

4 heaped tsp	green peppercorns
1 sliver	garlic
40g (1½oz)	butter
½ tsp	cinnamon or coriander
½ tsp	ground cumin and/or ginger
1	pheasant
	salt

Make a paste of 2 heaped tsp green peppercorns, garlic, butter and the spices. Lift the skin off the pheasant, and rub first the salt and then the paste well over the flesh, making a few gashes with a sharp knife in the legs so that the spices penetrate. Put a lump of the paste inside the pheasant and, if possible, leave for an hour or two before cooking.

Wrap the bird well in buttered paper or foil, and place in a moderate oven (180°C, 350°F, Gas Mark 4) for 45 minutes. Uncover the bird, add the remaining peppercorns to the juices, and cook for a further 15-30 minutes, basting frequently, until the skin is golden brown.

Serve the juices separately.

Serves 3-4

Green peppercorns in brine are available from good supermarkets. For a milder flavour, reduce the number used.

STIR-FRIED PHEASANT WITH GINGER AND APPLE

Prue Coats

	Flesh from 2 pheasants cut into thin strips
1 tbs	**sunflower oil**
2	**chunks preserved ginger, finely chopped,**
	plus 1 tbs of the syrup
1	**apple, cut into very thin strips**
1	**bunch spring onions, cut into strips**
150g (4oz)	**fresh bean sprouts**
	dash of soy sauce
	dash of rice vinegar
	salt and pepper
250g (9oz)	**packet of dried egg noodles**

Heat the oil in a wok or stir-fry pan. Put in the pheasant strips and the ginger and syrup, shake and stir for 1 minute. Push to one side of the pan and put in the apple and onion and let them caramelize. Meanwhile, cook the egg noodles in boiling water, according to the instructions on the packet, and drain. Add the bean sprouts and a dash of soy sauce and rice vinegar to the pheasant, apple and onion. Season to taste and mix in the egg noodles.

Serves 2-4

This is ideal for badly-shot birds.

MIDI PHEASANT

This works well with older birds.

1	large pheasant
3 tbs	olive oil
3-4	large onions, sliced
4-5	ripe tomatoes, skinned and chopped
1	red pepper, sliced
1	green pepper, sliced
2-3	courgettes, thickly sliced,
1	small, or ½ large aubergine,
	thickly sliced and cut into quarters
2-3	cloves garlic, crushed

Fry the onions in the oil until golden. Place them in a large casserole and lay the pheasant on top, breast downwards. Add the remaining ingredients and season with salt and freshly ground black pepper. Add a little water or suitable stock (the vegetables supply a good deal of the moisture), and cook slowly in the oven, with the lid on, for 3 hours, (150°C, 300°F, Gas Mark 2). For the last hour, turn the pheasant so the breast is upward.

Serve with potatoes or boiled rice.

Serves 4-6

PHEASANT WITH CELERY AND WALNUTS

1	pheasant
4	strips bacon
3 tbs	butter
	juice and rind of 2 oranges
75ml (3floz)	Madeira or port
	salt and pepper
75ml (3floz)	stock
1	celery heart, chopped
75g (3oz)	shelled walnuts

Melt 2 tbs of butter in a casserole and brown the pheasant all over. Cover the pheasant with the bacon, add the orange juice and Madeira or port, salt, pepper and stock. Cover with a lid and simmer gently for ¾-1 hour on the hob or cook in a moderate oven (180°C, 350°F, Gas Mark 4) for 1-1¼ hours.

Meanwhile trim the celery and cut into slices crossways. Heat the rest of the butter in a frying-pan, add the walnuts and celery, and toss over the heat with a pinch of salt, keeping the celery crisp. Put the shredded orange rinds in a pan of boiling water, and cook until tender, then drain and rinse.

Remove the pheasant from the oven and place on a serving dish; place the casserole on the hob and boil up the juices from the pheasant, thickening if necessary with a little cornflour mixed with water. Pour the sauce over the pheasant and serve with the celery, walnuts and orange rind scattered on the top.

Serves 3-4

PHEASANT IN CIDER AND APPLES

1	pheasant
3 tbs	butter
½	lemon
	a sprig of rosemary
6	Cox's apples, cored, peeled and sliced
½ tsp	cinnamon
½ tsp	celery salt
	ground pepper
275ml (½ pint)	dry cider
2 tbs	double cream or crème fraîche

Brown the pheasant in 2 tbs of the butter in a casserole, turning it over all the time. Take out and fill the inside with the lemon and a sprinkling of rosemary, together with the remaining juice and butter left in the casserole.

Wipe out the casserole, add the rest of the butter and fry the sliced apples. When slightly soft, sprinkle with cinnamon and return the pheasant to the casserole, breast-side down. Add the celery salt and pepper, and pour over the cider and cream or crème fraîche. Cover and cook in a moderate oven (180°C, 350°F, Gas Mark 4) for about an hour, or until the pheasant is cooked.

Joint the pheasant, bring the sauce to the boil and pour over the pieces of pheasant.

Serves 3-4

FAISAN AU RIZ BASQUAIS (PHEASANT WITH SPICED RICE)

Elizabeth David

1	large pheasant
350g(12oz)	Spanish chorizo, left whole
175-225g(6-8oz)	streaky bacon, preferably in one piece
	or a piece of boiling bacon
1	carrot, sliced
1	onion, sliced
	stock or water to cover
1	bouquet garni plus a small strip
	of orange peel
1	clove garlic, crushed
	pork, goose or duck dripping for frying
	(if not available, olive oil will do)
450g (1lb)	ripe tomatoes
3 or 4	sweet red peppers
	salt and pepper
1 dessertspoon	paprika

For the rice:

2 tbs	olive oil
350g (12oz)	long grain rice
900ml (1½ pints) stock or water	

Melt 2 tbs of the dripping or olive oil in a heavy saucepan large enough to hold the pheasant. Brown the sliced onion and carrot, then the pheasant, turning it over two or three times so that it colours evenly. Cover with half stock and half water, or all water. Put in the bacon in one piece, the bouquet garni, orange peel and the garlic; cover the pan. Simmer gently for 20 minutes, then add the chorizo and cook for a further half an hour.

To make the rice: heat 1 tbs oil gently in a solid-based saucepan or casserole. Tip the rice into the saucepan and stir the grains until they are thoroughly coated. Pour in the boiling stock or water and stir once as the liquid comes to simmering point. Put on a tight-fitting lid, turn the heat down low and leave for 15 minutes, when all the liquid should have been absorbed.

continued overleaf

In the meantime prepare the tomato and sweet pepper mixture. Skin and chop the tomatoes, remove the seeds and cores of the peppers, wash them and cut them into strips. Heat the remaining tablespoon of olive oil in a small saucepan or frying-pan, put in the tomatoes and sweet peppers and cook fairly briskly for about 10 minutes. Season with the salt, pepper and paprika. The mixture must be thick but not a purée.

To serve, turn the rice onto a heated dish. Extract the chorizo and the bacon from the saucepan. Slice the chorizo and remove the rind from the bacon and cut into squares. The pheasant may be either carved and arranged in the centre of the rice, or brought to the table whole and then carved. The chorizo and bacon are arranged round the pheasant, and the tomato and sweet pepper mixture in a ring round the rice.

Serves 3-4

PHEASANT WITH WILD RICE, CREAM AND HORSERADISH

2	pheasants
450ml (¾ pint)	chicken stock
1	onion
1	stick celery
1	bay leaf
1	carrot
8	rashers streaky bacon
2 tbs	butter
6-8	spring onions (depending on their size)
50ml (2fl oz)	brandy
	salt and pepper
100ml (4fl oz)	horseradish sauce
275ml (½ pint)	double cream
275ml (½ pint)	crème fraîche
175g (6oz)	cooked wild rice

Skin and quarter the pheasants, reserving the backs and necks. Place the backs and necks in the stock and add the onion, celery, bay leaf and carrot. Simmer fairly hard until it is reduced to about half, and strain.

Wrap the pheasant pieces in the bacon, secure with wooden toothpicks, then brown in butter with the chopped spring onions. When the pheasant pieces are brown, pour over the brandy and ignite. Transfer to a deep casserole, and pour over the strained stock. Season with salt and pepper, cover the casserole and place in a moderate oven (180°C, 350°F, Gas Mark 4) for half an hour, reducing the temperature to 160°C, 325°F, Gas Mark 3 for the remaining time, until the pheasant is tender – about 1-1½ hours.

Return the casserole to the hob, gently pull the toothpicks out of the meat and add horseradish, cream and crème fraîche, and cooked rice.

Serves 4-6

PHEASANT EN CROUTE
WITH REDCURRANT RELISH

1	pheasant
450ml (¾ pint)	stock
1	onion, finely chopped
2 tbs	butter
225g (8oz)	mushrooms, finely chopped
25-50g (1-2oz)	raisins
100g (4oz)	cooked rice
1 tsp	mixed herbs
350g (12oz)	puff pastry, bought or home-made
1	egg, beaten

For the relish:

1	red onion, finely chopped
3-4 tbs	good quality redcurrant jelly
2-3 tbs	fresh redcurrants (or fresh cranberries, according to season)
1	medium chilli, chopped

Place the pheasant in a heavy casserole and pour over the stock. Cook in a moderate oven (180°C, 350°F, Gas Mark 4) for 1-1½ hours. Remove from oven and, when cool, remove the meat from the carcass and cut into slices.

Melt the butter in a frying-pan and gently soften the onion; add the mushrooms and cook well. Stir in the raisins, cooked rice and mixed herbs; season well. Roll out the puff pastry into an oblong, about 20cm (8in) wide by 30cm (12in) deep, and place down the centre slices of pheasant sandwiched together with the rice stuffing. Fold up the pastry to resemble a large sausage roll, sealing the edges with beaten egg and decorate with left-over pastry pieces. Brush the whole with beaten egg and bake for 45 minutes in a hot oven (200°C, 400°F, Gas Mark 6).

To make the relish, gently warm the redcurrant jelly in a saucepan and stir in the chopped onion, chilli, redcurrants or cranberries. Cook for a few minutes.

Serves 3-4

STORE-CUPBOARD PHEASANT

2	pheasants, cut into joints
2 tbs	butter
1 tbs	oil
75ml (3oz)	finely chopped shallots
400g (14oz)	tin of tomatoes
1	clove garlic
	salt and pepper
½ tsp	thyme
	bouquet garni (4 sprigs parsley,
	1 celery top, 1 large bay leaf)
2	large strips lemon peel
150ml (¼ pint)	white wine
275ml (½ pint)	brown stock or tinned consommé
To garnish:	
225g (8oz)	mushrooms, sliced or
	1 small tin of mushrooms
	a few button onions
2 tbs	finely chopped parsley

Melt the butter and oil in a heavy pan or casserole and brown the pheasant pieces a few at a time. Remove from pan and keep warm. Cook the shallots in the remaining butter and oil, then stir in the tomatoes, garlic, salt, pepper, thyme, bouquet garni and lemon peel. Pour in the wine and stock.

Replace the pheasant in the casserole and cook slowly, with the lid on, for 1-1½ hours (160°C, 325°F, Gas Mark 3).

While this is cooking, sauté the mushrooms and button onions in the butter. When the pheasant is cooked, remove from the pan and skim off any surplus fat from the juices. Remove the bouquet garni and lemon peel and thicken the sauce, if necessary, with 1 tbs arrowroot or cornflour mixed with 2 tbs cold water. Reheat for 5 minutes, then serve on a hot platter. Surround the pheasant with mushrooms and onions, and sprinkle with parsley.

Serves 4-6

PHEASANT 'GUIDWIFE'

Prue Coats

Ideal for using up older pheasants.

1	pheasant
100g (4oz)	butter
4-5	large onions, preferably Spanish, peeled and sliced in thick rings
2-3 tbs	mango or peach chutney
	salt and pepper
275ml (½ pint)	stock
275ml (½ pint)	red wine
	beurre manié – optional

Melt the butter in a frying-pan and fry the onions until golden. Transfer to a casserole. Brown the pheasant in the remaining fat, then place on top of the onions. Spread the breast thickly with the chutney, season, then pour in the stock and wine to come halfway up the bird and put in a hot oven (200°C, 400°F, Gas Mark 6) for 1½ hours.

If a thick sauce is required, stir in a little beurre manié about half an hour before the end of the cooking time.

Serves 3-4

This recipe is equally good with pigeon.

DEVILLED PHEASANT

2 tsp	sugar
1 tsp	ground pepper
1 tsp	ginger
½ tsp	curry powder
½ tsp	mustard
2	pheasants cut into joints
50g (2oz)	melted butter
For the sauce:	
3 tbs	tomato chutney
1 tbs	Worcestershire sauce
1 tbs	soy sauce
2	dashes Tabasco
1 tbs	brown sauce, bought or home-made
	a little stock if necessary

Mix together the first five ingredients and rub them well into the pheasant joints. Leave for 1 hour, then brush the pheasant pieces with the melted butter and grill gently until brown and crisp, under a preheated grill (about 10 minutes each side). Meanwhile combine the sauce ingredients and heat gently in a small saucepan.

Put the pheasant joints on the bottom of a grill pan and spoon over the sauce. Continue cooking the birds under the grill, basting frequently, for about 15-20 minutes, then arrange them in a dish.

Dilute the sauce with stock if necessary, reheat and pour over the pheasants. Serve with rice.

Serves 4-6

Guinea-fowl and chicken can also be cooked in this way.

SAUTÉED PHEASANT WITH RED CABBAGE

1	pheasant, cut into joints
4 tbs	fat (lard, butter or bacon fat)
	a few juniper berries – optional
1	medium red cabbage
1	eating apple, peeled, cored and diced
	salt and pepper
275ml (½ pint)	single cream or crème fraîche
¼ tsp	paprika

Melt the fat in a heavy pan or casserole and brown the pheasant pieces and juniper berries, if using. Reduce the heat, cover and cook for 20 minutes.

Shred the cabbage finely and parboil in salted water for 10 minutes. Drain and add to the pheasant in the pan and allow to cook for another 10 minutes, along with the diced apple, covered. Add more salt and freshly-ground black pepper to taste, then add the cream or crème fraîche and simmer for 5 minutes. Sprinkle with paprika and serve with boiled potatoes.

Serves 3-4

This recipe works well with guinea-fowl or pigeon.

PHEASANT À LA GAYBIRD

2	onions, sliced
50g (2oz)	sultanas or grapes
4	pheasant breasts
4	glasses red wine
	salt and pepper
25g (1oz)	butter
275ml (½ pint)	double cream or crème fraîche

Take 4 large squares of foil and lay sliced onions in the centre of each. Sprinkle the sultanas or grapes over each bed of onion and place a pheasant breast on top. Gather up the edges of the foil, pour a glass of wine onto each pheasant breast, season, add a little butter and wrap into an airtight parcel. Cook in a very hot oven (230°C, 450°F, Gas Mark 8) for 30-35 minutes, depending on the size of the pheasants, then lower the heat to (110°C, 225°F, Gas Mark ¼) and cook for a further 1-1¼ hours.

Unwrap and remove the breasts. Tip the juices (except the cream) into a saucepan or frying-pan and cook until the liquid is reduced to 150ml (¼ pint). Season to taste.

Meanwhile slice the breasts, lay them in a dish, and cover to stop them getting dry. When the sauce is reduced, stir in the cream or crème fraîche and allow to boil for a few minutes until it thickens.

Pour the sauce over the meat and serve at once.

Serves 4

This recipe is equally delicious with grouse.

PHEASANT WITH PEPPERS AND ORANGES

2	pheasants cut into quarters
3 tbs	bacon fat or butter
2 tbs	Madeira or sherry
1 tsp	tomato purée
1 tsp	Bovril
1 tbs	plain flour
275ml (½ pint)	stock
	bouquet garni of parsley, bay leaf and thyme
	salt and pepper
2 tbs	olive oil
1	clove garlic, crushed
100g (4oz)	mushrooms, sliced
½	red pepper, diced
½	green pepper, diced
3	tomatoes, skinned, seeded and coarsely chopped
	grated rind of 1 orange
2	oranges, peeled, skinned and sliced very thinly

Brown the pheasants in butter or bacon fat in a large frying-pan or casserole; pour over the Madeira or sherry. Remove the pheasants, then add the tomato purée, Bovril and flour to the pan. Stir very well and gradually pour in the stock.

Stir until the mixture comes to a boil, put the pheasants back in the pan, then add the bouquet garni, salt and pepper.

Cover and cook slowly in a moderate oven (180°C, 350°F, Gas Mark 4) for about 45 minutes. Remove bouquet garni and arrange pheasants on a warm platter.

In a separate pan, heat the olive oil, add the garlic, and cook for a minute, then add the mushrooms, peppers, tomatoes and orange rind. Cook gently for several minutes then add the sauce in which the pheasants were cooked. Finally add the sliced oranges and as soon as they are warm, pour the sauce over the pheasant.

Serves 4-6

PHEASANT WITH ROSTI

4	pheasant breasts, skinned
4	slices bacon
2 tbs	lard, oil or bacon fat
I	small onion, chopped
2-3	potatoes, coarsely grated
	freshly ground pepper
2-3	juniper berries, crushed

Wrap the pheasant breasts in bacon, securing with toothpicks. Brown the pheasant in lard, oil or bacon fat, remove from the pan and sauté the onion in the remaining fat. When the onion is slightly brown, add the potatoes, lots of pepper and the juniper berries and stir well. Place the potato mixture in a buttered shallow casserole and put the pheasant pieces on top. Cover the casserole and place in moderate oven, (180°C, 350°F, Gas Mark 4) for 30 minutes.

Serves 4

PHEASANT IN A RICH RED WINE SAUCE

1	young pheasant
150ml (¼ pint)	red wine
450ml (¾ pint)	strong game stock
1 tbs	good quality redcurrant jelly
5 tbs	brandy
2 tbs	Dijon mustard
	juice of ½ lemon
225g (8oz)	chicken livers, lightly sautéed

Roast the pheasant in a moderate oven (180°C, 350°F, Gas Mark 4), basting as often as possible, for 1 hour, or use a roasting pan with lid or a roasting bag (follow the instructions given on the packet).

Carve into serving pieces and keep warm.

In a frying-pan, reduce the red wine and stock to about 150ml (¼ pint). Whisk in the redcurrant jelly until melted, add the brandy and mustard, whisking all the time, then add the lemon juice and finally the chicken livers. When the sauce is smooth and bubbling, place the pheasant in the pan and heat in the sauce for 5 minutes.

PHEASANTS WITH APPLE PURÉE

100g (4oz)	lardons
1	onion, finely chopped
1	clove garlic, crushed
2 tbs	butter
2 tbs	oil
1	pheasant
350g (12oz)	hard cooking apples
2 tbs	Calvados, brandy or whisky
275ml (½ pint)	cream or crème fraîche
	salt and pepper

Lightly fry the lardons, onion and garlic in the butter and oil in a heavy casserole. Remove with a slotted spoon. Brown the pheasant all over in the fat, turning frequently, then remove and keep warm. Peel, core and slice the apples and add them to the fat. Cook until they start to turn golden. Pour over the Calvados (or brandy or whisky) and skim the fat from the pan juices. Put the pheasant back in the casserole and surround with apples, lardons , onion and garlic. Bring to a simmer, stir in the cream or crème fraîche, salt and pepper, then cover the casserole and cook in a moderately cool oven (160°C, 325°F, Gas Mark 3) until tender, about 1½ hours. When ready, remove the pheasant and the lardons, and purée the remaining sauce. Check for seasoning and serve.

Serves 3-4

PHEASANT IN GIN

2	pheasants
4-6	juniper berries
75ml (2½ floz)	gin
75ml (2½ floz)	hot water
To serve:	apple sauce (1 large cooking apple, peeled, cored and diced, poached in a little water and sweetened to taste)

Place 2-3 crushed juniper berries inside each bird.

Put the birds in a very hot oven (230°C, 450°F, Gas Mark 8) for 10 minutes, then reduce to (200°C, 400°F, Gas Mark 6) and roast, basting frequently with the gin and hot water, until cooked – about 35 minutes.

Serve with the strained juices as a gravy and with the apple sauce.

Serves 4-6

BREAST OF PHEASANT
WITH HAM & MUSHROOMS

2	thin slices of ham
4 tbs	butter
2	pheasant breasts
	salt and pepper
4	mushroom caps
2	slices toast
1 tsp	flour
4-6 tbs	sherry or Madeira

Sauté the pheasant breasts in the butter, add salt, pepper and mushrooms, and cook for 15 minutes, turning frequently and basting with the pan juices. Warm the ham in the pan juices, then, in a serving dish, place the ham on the toast, put the pheasant on the ham and top with mushrooms. Stir a little flour into the pan juices, allow to boil and add the Madeira or sherry, stirring all the time. When it is boiling, pour over the pheasant. Serve this with rice cooked with a little sautéed onion.

Serves 2

Optional: Place a thin slice of mozzarella cheese on the ham and, after pouring over the sauce, place the dish under the grill until the cheese melts and bubbles.

HOBNAIL PHEASANT

A good recipe for an old cock pheasant with spurs like hobnails and as tough as old boots!

1	old pheasant
50g (2oz)	butter
2	large cooking apples, peeled, cored and sliced
50ml (2oz)	Calvados
100ml (4oz)	single cream

Put the pheasant in a colander over a pan of gently boiling water for 15-20 minutes to tenderize it.

Melt the butter in a heavy casserole and brown the bird on all sides. Put the apple slices under and around the bird, cover the casserole and cook in a medium oven (180°C, 350°F, Gas Mark 4) for 30-40 minutes according to the size of the bird.

Remove the bird from the casserole and keep warm; pour into the casserole containing the apples, butter and cooking juices, the Calvados and cream. Stir well with a wooden spoon to a smooth consistency (do not boil – the residual heat of the heavy iron pan is enough).

Carve the bird and serve the sauce separately.

If using a young bird the steaming process is unnecessary.

Serves 3-4

PARTRIDGE

Partridge have a subtle flavour and, in the case of young birds, are best served simply roasted, pan-fried or grilled. There are two species in Britain – the native grey, often called the English, partridge *(Perdix perdix)* and the French or red-legged *(Alectoris rufa)*. They are small birds and one will usually serve only one person, though larger birds may be enough for two. The open season for partridge shooting runs from September 1 to February 1, with October and November being the best time for eating this delicious little gamebird. Greys are often considered the superior of the two, from a table, as well as a sporting perspective, but numbers have been declining for many decades because of agricultural intensification and only areas that are actively keepered for wild partridge shooting are likely to produce a shootable surplus.

The red-legged, on the other hand, has a stable population. Birds need little or no hanging early in the season when the weather is warm; later on, three to five days is about right, according to personal taste. Birds must always be hung in a cool, fly-proof environment.

Fresh or frozen oven-ready birds are available from most game dealers.

For preparation details, see page 270.

Wine recommendation

The most appropriate accompaniment for partridge is Gevrey-Chambertin, however a mature Merlot-dominated Pomerol or St Emilion will do the job equally well. When partridge is served with apples and Calvados, the wine choice is more tricky. Try a Barbera from Italy or even a full-bodied Burgundy such as Meursault.

ROAST PARTRIDGE

2   partridge

15g (½oz)   butter, seasoned with salt and pepper

2   thin strips of pork fat or streaky bacon

           a few drops of balsamic vinegar

           giblet gravy

Put half the seasoned butter inside each bird and tie pork fat or bacon over the breast. Place on a trivet or rack in a roasting tin and cook, breast down, in a moderately hot oven (200°C, 400°F, Gas Mark 6), for 10 minutes, reducing the oven temperature to (180°C, 350°F, Gas Mark 4) for a further 30-35 minutes, basting frequently with melted butter. 15 minutes before the end of the cooking time, remove the fat and turn the birds over to allow the breasts to brown. Remove the birds from the roasting tin and keep warm.

Skim the excess fat from the pan juices and reduce to make a thin gravy – add vegetable water and a little stock if necessary. A few drops of balsamic vinegar will improve the flavour of the gravy. Serve with game chips and bread sauce (see pages 255 and 238)

Serves 2

Gamebirds cook well in a lidded roasting pan in which case there is no need to baste.

GRILLED PARTRIDGE

Only use tender young partridge for this dish and allow time for the grill to get very hot.

2	young partridge
2 tbs	butter
	salt and pepper
	bunch of watercress
1	lemon

Split the partridge down the back and force the halves apart until they are flat. Skewer them open or cut them completely in half if preferred. Rub them all over very well with the softened butter and season with salt and pepper. Cook under a hot grill, being careful not to let them burn, and turn them several times, brushing with more butter. Do not overcook them – about 10-15 minutes should be long enough.

Serve with watercress and lemon wedges.

Serves 2

Young partridge can also be cooked on the barbecue.

PARTRIDGE
WITH CABBAGE

1	medium-sized hard cabbage
100g (4oz)	piece uncooked ham or lean bacon
2	partridge
3 tbs	butter or bacon fat
2	small onions
2	cloves
2	carrots
2	small smoked sausages (or cocktail frankfurters or 100g/4oz garlic sausage)
2-3	crushed juniper berries
	salt and pepper
	a scraping of nutmeg
450ml (¾ pint)	well-flavoured stock

Cut the cabbage into fine slices and parboil in boiling salted water for 7 minutes. Drain carefully and press out all the water. Blanch the bacon or ham if salty and cut into slices. Brown the birds in the butter or bacon fat, and place a small onion with a clove stuck into it inside each bird. Put a layer of cabbage in a deep casserole, lay the partridge on top, then the ham, sliced carrots, sausages, juniper berries, salt, pepper and nutmeg. Cover with the rest of the cabbage, pour over the stock to about halfway up, cover with foil and the lid, and cook in a cool oven (140°C, 275°F, Mark 1) for 3-4 hours.

The gravy may need to be thickened slightly or reduced.

Serves 2-3

CASSEROLED PARTRIDGE WITH RED WINE AND MUSHROOMS

225g (8oz)	streaky bacon
3	partridge
225g (8oz)	button onions or shallots
225g (8oz)	button mushrooms (reserve trimmings)
150ml (¼ pint)	red wine
900ml (1½ pints)	stock
	bouquet garni
25g (1oz)	vegetable fat or oil
1	small onion, finely chopped
l tbs	flour
	salt and pepper
1 tbs	chopped parsley

Dice the bacon and cook half of it in a heavy saucepan until the fat runs. Add the partridge and brown them all over. Take the pan off the heat and add the whole onions and mushrooms. Pour over the red wine and 275ml (½ pint) of the stock and add the bouquet garni. Place in the centre of a moderately slow oven (170°C, 325°F, Gas Mark 3) for 2-2½ hours.

Meanwhile heat the remaining pieces of bacon in a frying-pan in vegetable fat or oil, add the chopped onion and cook gently until soft. Add the flour, continue to cook gently until the roux is dark brown in colour (about 15 minutes). Stir in the remaining stock, a little at a time, and bring to the boil, stirring all the time. Add the mushroom trimmings. Simmer for 30 minutes, thinning with stock if necessary. Season to taste.

When the partridge is cooked, remove from the casserole and strain the liquid off. Cut the birds in half, remove the breast and leg section from the carcass. Replace these in the casserole. Pour the sauce over the birds, sprinkle with parsley and serve.

Serves 4-6

STIR-FRIED PARTRIDGE BREASTS
WITH MUSHROOMS & CREAM

4	partridge breasts, skinned
1	red onion, sliced
(100g) 4oz	mushrooms, sliced
	oil for frying
3-4 tbs	double cream or crème fraîche
	a little stock

Thinly slice the breasts across the grain of the meat and stir fry in the hot oil with the onion and mushrooms. When the meat has browned all over (2-3 minutes) add a little stock to make a gravy and stir well. Simmer for a further 2-3 minutes. Add the cream or crème fraîche to thicken and serve immediately with rice, noodles or new potatoes.

Serves 2-3

PARTRIDGE WITH ONIONS AND CREAM

2	partridge
2	large onions, sliced
150ml (¼ pint)	stock
50g (2oz)	butter
	salt and pepper
4 tbs	double cream

Place the partridge in a deep casserole. Surround with sliced onions, stock, butter and seasoning.

Cover, and put in a moderately slow oven (170°C, 325°F, Gas Mark 3) for 1½-2 hours.

Lift out the birds and split in two down the backbone.

Liquidize the onions and the rest of the casserole contents and add the cream.

Reheat gently and spoon over the birds.

Serves 3-4

PERDRIX À LA PURÉE DE LENTILLES
(PARTRIDGE WITH LENTILS)
Elizabeth David

6	partridge
75-100g (3-4 oz)	butter,
1	large onion, sliced
2	carrots, cut in rounds
	a glass of white wine
	salt and pepper
150ml (5fl oz)	good game stock

For the purée:

450g (1lb)	brown lentils,
1	onion stuck with 2 cloves
2	cloves garlic
2	carrots, sliced
	salt

Melt the butter in a pan or casserole just large enough to hold the partridge and add the birds, onion and carrot. When the birds start to brown, pour over a glass of white wine and let it reduce by half; then add the seasoning and the stock, cover the pan and finish cooking either over a very low flame or in a moderately slow oven (170°C, 325°F, Gas Mark 3) for about 1½-2 hours. The exact time depends upon the size and age of the partridge.

Meanwhile, place the brown lentils, onion stuck with cloves, garlic and carrots in a large saucepan, cover with water, bring to the boil and simmer for 2 hours. When the lentils are quite soft put them through a sieve (or purée in a food processor or liquidizer) and season to taste.

In another saucepan mix the purée with half the sauce from the partridge, and cook over a medium heat, stirring all the time, until the purée is smooth and of the right consistency.

Serve the partridge on a dish, with the purée all round and the rest of the sauce poured over.

Serves 6

PARTRIDGE IN WHITE WINE

25g (1oz)	butter
50g (2oz)	streaky bacon, cut into small pieces
2	partridge
3 tbs	brandy (optional)
100ml (4fl oz)	white wine
75ml (3fl oz)	chicken stock
	bouquet garni

Melt the butter in a casserole just big enough to hold the birds. Start to cook the bacon, then add the partridge and brown lightly all over. Add the brandy, if using, then add the wine, stock and bouquet garni. Cover very tightly, bring to the boil and place in moderately slow oven (170°C, 325°F, Gas Mark 3) for about 1½-2 hours.

When cooked, reduce the sauce until it just coats the back of a spoon, then pour over the birds.

Serves 2-3

PERDRIX À LA CATALANE

Elizabeth David

4	partridge
2 tbs	pork or bacon fat,
	or a mixture of oil and butter
	salt and pepper
2 tbs	flour
2	glasses white wine (not too dry)
1	small glass port
2	red peppers, cut into strips
24	cloves garlic
2	oranges (preferably Seville)
570ml (1 pint)	water

Melt the pork or bacon fat or mixture of oil and butter in a heavy pan just large enough to hold the partridge. Brown the birds all over and season with salt and pepper. Sprinkle with the flour, and stir until the flour and the fat have amalgamated and turned golden.

Pour over the white wine and port. Add a little water until the liquid comes just over halfway up the partridge.

Cover the pan and simmer over a low heat for 2-3 hours (depending on the size and age of the birds) or in a moderately cool oven (170°C, 325°F, Gas Mark 3) for about 2 hours. Halfway through the cooking time, add the red pepper. In the meantime peel 24 cloves of garlic and cut one of the oranges into slices, rind included; put these into a pint of water and cook until the water boils. This removes the bitterness from the orange and the garlic, which are then strained and put into a second pan of water and cooked for another 8-10 minutes. The garlic will now taste very mild, but for a stronger garlic flavour this second cooking can be omitted.

By this time the liquid will be considerably reduced and the whole mixture is added to the partridge, together with the juice of a second orange, and all cooked together for another 10-15 minutes, until the partridge are tender. If the sauce is not thick enough, take the partridge out and keep them hot, turn up the flame and let the sauce bubble until it is sufficiently reduced.

Serve the partridge surrounded with the sauce, peppers, orange and garlic.

Serves 4-6

PARTRIDGE WITH RED CABBAGE AND CHESTNUTS

25g (1oz)	bacon fat, dripping or butter
50g (2oz)	streaky bacon, cut into small pieces
2	partridge
1	small red cabbage
1	eating apple, peeled, cored and diced
	or 3tbs cassis
225g (8oz)	chestnuts, peeled (fresh, tinned
	or vacuum-packed)
	salt and pepper
225ml (8fl oz)	still, dry cider

Melt the fat in a casserole and brown the bacon pieces. Remove, and brown the partridge all over. Wash the cabbage, shred it, place half in the bottom of the casserole together with the apple or cassis, then the partridge, bacon and chestnuts*, salt and pepper. Cover with the remaining cabbage and pour over the cider.

Cover the casserole tightly and place in a moderately slow oven (170°C, 325°F, Gas Mark 3) for 1½-2 hours.

Serves 2-3

*If using pre-cooked chestnuts, add to the casserole for the final half hour only.

YOUNG PARTRIDGE
WITH GRAPES

3	young partridge
4 tbs	butter
	salt and pepper
3	slices pork fat or streaky bacon
3 or 6	croutons
100ml (4fl oz)	dry white wine
75ml (3fl oz)	game stock
225g (8oz)	seedless grapes

Spread about 1 tbs butter over each bird, sprinkle with salt and pepper, place a slice of pork fat or bacon over each breast and roast the birds in a hot oven (200°C, 400°F, Gas Mark 6) for about 30 minutes, basting occasionally.

Remove the pork or bacon slices and set aside, then place the birds back in the oven until the breasts are browned, about 5 minutes. Depending on their size, serve each bird whole on a crouton (larger birds can be split in half) and place on a warm serving dish.

Pour off any fat from the roasting pan, then add the wine, stock and about half the grapes to the pan, and cook for 4 minutes, stirring well. Add the remaining butter and cook for a minute. Put the slices of bacon or pork fat back on the birds and place a few small bunches of grapes around the platter. Serve the sauce separately.

Serves 3-6

GREEK PARTRIDGE

4	partridge (retain livers and giblets if possible)
2 tbs	olive oil
2	cloves garlic
	salt
	pinch of cayenne
	sprig of rosemary
4-8	vine leaves, depending on size
75-100g (3-4oz)	mushrooms
50g (2oz)	butter
	a little dry white wine

Brush the birds with the olive oil, rub with garlic and dust with salt and cayenne. Place a piece of rosemary in each. Wrap them in one or two vine leaves, securing with wooden toothpicks. Chop the livers and giblets with equal amounts of mushrooms, and sauté in butter until half cooked. Stir in the dry white wine to make enough basting liquid.

Butter the casserole, put in the birds and the liquid, cover very well with foil and the lid, and cook for 45 minutes in a moderate oven (180°C, 350°F, Gas Mark 4). Remove the birds when cooked, and boil the gravy to reduce it.

Serves 4

HUNGARIAN PARTRIDGE

4	partridge
	salt
	olive oil
2-3	crushed juniper berries per bird
75ml (3fl oz)	red wine
1½ tsp	finely grated onion
	a pinch of cayenne
40g (1½oz)	chopped almonds
50g (2oz)	halved Muscat grapes or fat raisins

Rub the birds inside and out with salt, brush with olive oil and place the juniper berries inside. Make a basting liquid by mixing the red wine, grated onion, salt, cayenne, almonds and grapes or raisins. Roast the birds in a hot oven (200°C, 400°F, Gas Mark 6), breast down, and pour over the basting liquid. Baste frequently until cooked, about 40 minutes. Turn the birds over to brown the breasts 10 minutes before the end of the cooking time. Remove the birds and keep warm; reduce the liquid and thicken slightly if necessary. Pour over the birds.

Serves 4

BENTLEY COLD PARTRIDGE

25g (1oz)	butter
1	partridge
570ml (1 pint)	jellied stock (home-made or bought)
2 tbs	sherry

Put the butter inside the partridge. Place in a casserole and cover with jellied stock. Add the sherry and cook very slowly on the hob for about two hours. It is important that the casserole has a very tight-fitting lid or tin foil between the lid and pot. Leave to cool and set.

When ready to eat, remove the meat from the carcass and cut into slices. Serve with a salad of lettuce and pears stuffed with cream cheese.

Serves 1-2

PARTRIDGE WITH APPLES

2	young partridge
	livers from partridge, or small quantity
	of liver paté
4 tbs	butter
	salt and pepper
2	sweet hard apples
2	slices bread
4 tbs	Calvados or whisky
1	bunch watercress

Cover the partridges with half the butter and season with salt and pepper. Place in a pan with enough water in it to cover the bottom, and roast in a moderate oven (180°C, 350°F, Gas Mark 4) for 30 minutes.

Peel the apples, remove the cores and cut in half. Place them on a buttered baking dish, flat side down. Dot them with ½ tbs butter and place in the oven until they are just cooked, about half an hour, or melt the butter in a frying-pan and fry the apples for 5-10 minutes.

Sauté the bread in 1 tbs butter and spread with a paste made from the sautéed partridge livers and ½ tbs butter (or a small amount of liver paté). Arrange the partridge on the crouton on a hot platter. Blend the juices in the pan with the Calvados or whisky, ignite, and shake the pan until the flame goes out. Pour this over the partridge and surround with the apples and watercress.

Serves 2

GROUSE

In a culinary context, the word grouse generally means the red grouse; these little birds inhabit the heather-clad moorlands of upland Britain and provide testing sport from August 12th when the season opens (the famous Glorious Twelfth) until December 10th.

Grouse have a distinctive flavour and for many are regarded as the aristocrats of gamebirds and, as such, are treated with great reverence. They are best served fairly simply so as not to obscure the true taste of the meat – one bird is generally sufficient for one person. Other species of grouse include the ptarmigan, black grouse and the capercaillie. Opinion varies as to the gastronomic value of these latter two birds and they are generally used in pâtés or pies, but the ptarmigan makes very good eating and can be roasted, casseroled or spatchcocked (split open and grilled) in the same way as the red grouse. Grouse are often eaten without hanging, especially those shot at the beginning of the season when the weather is warm. But if a stronger flavour is desired they can be hung for 2-4 days depending on the weather – they will keep far longer if it is cool. Hang them where the air can circulate, preferably not touching each other, and ensure that the area is completely fly-proof. If birds have become clammy from travelling in cars, or are a little "high", they can be dipped in vinegar or Milton sterilizing fluid after plucking. Fresh oven-ready grouse are available from certain gamedealers and butchers during the shooting season; when out of season, frozen birds can be bought.

For preparation details see page 270.

Wine recommendation

Although Pinot Noir is the ideal accompaniment for many game recipes, a Ribeira del Duero from Spain would be a good alternative for grouse. Failing that, the very finest of red burgundies from the Côte de Nuits would also be ideal.

ROAST YOUNG GROUSE

2	young grouse
50g (2oz)	seasoned butter
2	slices bacon
2	slices white bread (sautéed in butter)

Insert a piece of seasoned butter into each bird and cover the breasts with bacon. Place on the sautéed bread and put into a roasting tin in a moderately hot oven (190°C, 375°F, Gas Mark 5) for 35-40 minutes, depending on the size of the grouse. Baste frequently. Remove the bacon 10 minutes before the bird is ready to allow the breast to brown.

Serve with bread sauce, fried breadcrumbs, game chips or crisps, and gravy, (see pages 238, 264, 255)

Serves 2

Grouse are often served on a crouton of bread fried in butter on which the mashed and sautéed liver of the bird has been spread. This may be put under the bird during part of the cooking to catch the juices, or when serving.

GRILLED SPATCHCOCK GROUSE

Only the best young grouse should be grilled or barbecued

1	young grouse
1 tbs	butter
	salt and pepper
2-3	juniper berries, crushed (optional)

Split the grouse down the back and force the halves apart until they are flat. Then skewer them open. Rub them well with softened butter and season with plenty of salt and pepper and a few crushed juniper berries, if using.

Grill under a high heat, turning occasionally, and brushing with more butter if necessary. Be careful not to overcook – 8-10 minutes each side is about right. If preferred the birds can be cut completely in half, but this is more inclined to let the juices run out of the breasts.

Serves 1

To barbecue grouse, brush the spatchcocked bird with olive oil and season with salt and pepper. Cook over the coals, basting all the time, taking care that they do not burn. This should take about 15 minutes. Serve with barbecue sauce (see page 240)

GROUSE PARCELS

Angela Humphreys

2	young grouse
4	rashers bacon
2 tbs	cranberry or rowanberry jelly, see page 269

Split the grouse in halves using game shears or kitchen scissors, trim off any loose bones and wash thoroughly in cold water, removing any loose pellets under the skin and any remaining innards.

Place each half, flesh-side up, on a square of tin foil. Add a rasher of bacon and ½ tbs of jelly to each. Wrap and seal the foil parcel. Cook on a barbecue or in a moderate oven (180°C, 350°F, Gas Mark 4) for 20-30 minutes.

Serve with crusty bread and salads.

Serves 4

GROUSE À LA CRÈME

2	young grouse
	salt and pepper
50g (2oz)	butter
275ml (½ pint)	double cream
2 tbs	brandy

Season the grouse, cover with half of the butter, and cook in a heavy casserole in a moderate oven (180°C, 350°F, Gas Mark 4) for about 35-40 minutes. When the grouse is cooked, remove from the casserole and keep warm; pour out the surplus butter, add the brandy and bring to the boil. Add the cream and bring to the boil once more. Stir in the remainder of the butter and season to taste. Remove the string from the grouse, cut in halves if desired, and pour over the sauce.

Serves 2

Mushrooms can also be added to this dish.

GROUSE AU VIN

2	grouse
100g (4oz)	lardons
3-4 tbs	butter
	salt and pepper
100ml (4floz)	brandy
570ml (1 pint)	red wine
275ml (½ pint)	grouse or chicken stock
	or tinned consommé
½ tbs	tomato purée
1	clove garlic, crushed
¼ tsp	thyme
1	bay leaf
10	button onions
225g (8oz)	mushrooms
1 tbs	cornflour
1 tbs	chopped parsley

Cut the grouse into serving pieces. Fry the lardons in a knob of butter until golden and remove to a plate. Fry the grouse in the same pan and, when brown, return the lardons to the pan; season, cover, and cook slowly for 10 minutes. Add the brandy, ignite, and shake the pan until the flames die out. Add the wine, stock, tomato purée, garlic and herbs.

Cover, and simmer slowly for 30-50 minutes depending on the age of the grouse.

Meanwhile sauté the onions and then the mushrooms in butter until golden. Remove the grouse, skim off the fat from the liquid and then reduce the liquid to 570ml (1 pint). Check for seasoning.

Thicken the sauce with the cornflour mixed with a little water. Serve from the casserole, placing the mushrooms and onions around the edge. Sprinkle the top with the parsley.

MARINATED GROUSE WITH ALMONDS

4	young grouse

For the marinade:

1	clove garlic, crushed
1 tbs	olive oil
1 tbs	lemon juice
	salt and pepper

75g (3oz)	butter
50-75g (2-3oz)	flaked almonds
2 tbs	lemon juice
½ tsp	finely grated lemon rind
1 tbs	freshly chopped parsley
To garnish:	parsley sprigs and fried croutons

Split the grouse down the back and force the halves apart until they are flat. Combine the marinade ingredients, pour over the grouse and leave for about ½-1 hour.

Place the grouse on a grill rack lined with foil and cook under a moderate heat until well browned – about 15-20 minutes. Turn the grouse halfway through the cooking time and baste with the marinade.

Meanwhile fry the almonds in the melted butter until golden brown. Add the 2 tbs of lemon juice and remove from the heat. Season and stir in the lemon rind and chopped parsley. Transfer the grouse to a warm serving dish and spoon over the almond mixture.

Garnish with fried croutons and parsley.

Serves 4

FRIED GROUSE WITH BLACKCURRANT SAUCE

2	grouse
2 tbs	butter or margarine
	salt and pepper
5	slices carrot
1	small onion
5	juniper berries, crushed
150ml (¼ pint)	red wine
150ml (¼ pint)	beef broth or water
150ml (¼ pint)	cream
2 tbs	arrowroot or cornflour
1 tsp	blackcurrant jelly
1 tbs	brandy – optional

Heat the butter or margarine in a pan and fry the birds. Add salt, pepper, carrot, onion cut into four and juniper berries. Add the wine and beef broth or water, then cover and let simmer slowly until the birds are tender, about 30-40 minutes. Take out the birds and keep them hot while making the sauce.

Strain the gravy, add the cream and bring to the boil. Add the arrowroot or cornflour dissolved in a little water, blackcurrant jelly and the brandy, if using.

Cut the birds into halves and put them on a serving plate, serving the sauce separately.

Serve with small fried potato cubes, extra blackcurrant jelly and salad.

Serves 2

MALTED GROUSE

Angela Humphreys

2	grouse
570ml (1 pint)	chicken stock
1	small onion finely sliced
1	large carrot sliced
2 tbs	whisky
225g (8oz)	mushrooms, chopped
	chopped parsley

Place the grouse, onion, carrot and stock in a saucepan, bring to the boil and simmer for 1 hour (or cook in a pressure-cooker for 30 minutes).

Remove the birds from the pan, and when cool enough to handle, split in half and trim from the rib-bones. Place the halves in a casserole, liquidize the softened vegetables or pass through a sieve, and add to the casserole along with the remaining stock. Add the chopped mushrooms, parsley and whisky. Cover and cook in a moderate oven (180°C, 350°F, Gas Mark 4) for a further hour.

Serves 2

This recipe is suitable for older grouse

DUNTREATH ROAST GROUSE

2	grouse
2 tbs	butter
½	apple
6-8	slices streaky bacon

Place a knob of butter and a piece of apple inside each bird and completely wrap in streaky bacon.

Stand the birds in 1cm (½in) water in a roasting pan, cover with greaseproof paper, then cover with a lid or large sheet of foil and cook in a moderate oven (180°C, 350°F, Gas Mark 4) for 15 minutes, reducing to a slow oven (150°C, 300°F, Gas Mark 2) for ¾-1 hour.

Serve with gravy made from the pan juices.

Serves 2

EGGLESTON GROUSE

1	brace grouse
2	rashers bacon
50g (2oz)	butter
75-100ml(3-4fl oz)	hollandaise sauce
	(bought or home-made,
	see page 246)

For the béchamel sauce:

275ml (½ pint)	milk
½	bay leaf
1	blade mace
1	slice onion
6	peppercorns
15g (½oz)	butter
15g (½oz)	flour

For the accompanying salad:

100g (4oz)	cooked rice
1	carrot, diced
2	sticks celery, diced
8	walnuts, quartered
	French dressing

Place the bacon on the breasts of the grouse and place a quarter of the butter inside each; put the rest of the butter in the roasting tin with the birds. Roast in a hot oven (200°C, 400°F, Gas Mark 6) for about 40 minutes or until cooked.

Allow to cool. Meanwhile prepare the béchamel sauce. Put the bay leaf, mace, onion, peppercorns and milk in a saucepan, bring to the boil, remove the pan from the heat, cover tightly and leave to infuse for 15-20 minutes.

In a separate pan, melt the butter, blend in the flour to make a roux and stir in the strained infused milk, a little at a time, until boiling. Add a little of the béchamel sauce to the hollandaise sauce and then add this to the main bulk of the béchamel and beat until cool. Season the sauce and set aside. Skin and shred the grouse and arrange at one end of an oval serving dish. Coat with the sauce and reserve the rest to serve separately. At the other end of the dish arrange the salad, which is made by mixing all the ingredients together and binding with a little French dressing.

Garnish the dish with a dusting of paprika pepper.

Serves 4 as part of a buffet

SALMIS OF GROUSE

2	young grouse
2 tbs	softened butter
275ml (½ pint)	good quality game stock
2	onions, chopped
2	carrots, chopped
1	clove garlic, crushed
2 tbs	butter
1 tbs	flour
75ml (3fl oz)	red wine
1 tbs	tomato purée
	a pinch of thyme
1	bay leaf
	salt and pepper
5-10	button onions
5-10	mushrooms, sliced
To serve:	croutons and 1 tbs chopped parsley

Rub the softened butter over the birds and roast in a moderate oven (180°C, 350°F, Gas Mark 4) for 20 minutes, until half cooked.

Remove from the oven and allow to cool slightly, then either cut them into serving pieces, remembering to catch all the juices on a plate, or remove the legs and gently pull the rest of the meat away from the carcass. Keep warm. Crush the carcass and simmer in the stock.

Meanwhile, sauté the onions, carrots and garlic in the 2 tbs of butter in a shallow, heatproof oven dish. Stir in the flour, then slowly add the red wine, stock, tomato purée, thyme, bay leaf, salt and pepper, and simmer for about an hour. Thicken a little more if necessary.

In a separate pan, sauté the sliced mushrooms, onions and croutons of bread. Place the mushrooms and onions over the grouse and strain the juices over the meat. Heat very slowly, never allowing it to bubble, until the grouse is cooked through, about 15 minutes. Surround with chopped parsley and croutons.

Serves 2

WOODCOCK & SNIPE

While each has its own distinctive flavour, woodcock and snipe have much in common from a gastronomic viewpoint and a recipe that works for one will work equally well for the other. The traditional way to eat them is ungutted, that is complete with their entrails. As the bird cooks the entrails – or trail – liquefy and form part of the juices. Another custom is to leave the head on and use the long bill as a skewer to truss the bird.

For many, the woodcock is considered to have the best flavour of all Britain's gamebirds. An average bird will serve one person, whereas two snipe will be needed for a single serving as one bird has only about 2oz of meat on it.

Only the common snipe may be shot in Britain, the Jack Snipe being a protected species.

Woodcock and snipe may be hung for anything from 5-10 days, but this is a matter of personal choice. Some people who like to eat the whole bird say that hanging can spoil the taste of the trail and prefer not to hang at all.

Both are much prized in the sporting field and most Guns will take them home to eat, so they are rarely on sale at gamedealers or butchers.

For details of how to prepare woodcock and snipe, see page 270.

Wine recommendation

These smaller gamebirds are most perfectly suited to younger Pinot Noirs which are more tannic and have a hint of rusticity about them. A Pommard would be well suited, however the longer they are hung the more they require a bigger wine such as a good Claret.

ROAST WOODCOCK

2	woodcock, gizzards removed
2 tbs	butter
2	slices of bacon
2	croutons
	salt and pepper
	squeeze of lemon juice
	a few drops of brandy
	lemon wedges

Cover the bird generously with softened butter and place a slice of bacon over the breast. Place in a very hot oven (220°C, 425°F, Gas Mark 7) for 10-15 minutes, according to the size of the bird and personal taste.

Either serve simply on a crouton fried in butter or extract the entrails and mash them up with some salt, pepper, lemon juice and a few drops of brandy, and spread this on the crouton underneath the woodcock.

Serve with lemon wedges.

Serves 2

WOODCOCK WITH FRIED CRUMBS

1	woodcock – retain liver and heart
	butter
	salt and pepper
1	piece of toast
1	shallot, chopped
25g (1oz)	breadcrumbs

Carefully gut the woodcock, removing the gizzard and retaining the liver and heart. Put the trail back in.

Put a little butter inside and sprinkle with salt and pepper inside and out. Roast in a very hot oven (220°C, 425°F, Gas Mark 7) for 10-15 minutes, according to the size of the bird and personal taste.

Meanwhile, dice the liver and heart and fry, together with the chopped shallot, in a little butter. Add the breadcrumbs and fry until golden. When the woodcock is cooked, serve on a hot slice of toast with the juices poured over and the crumbs alongside.

Serves 1

COLD WOODCOCK

WOODCOCK EN COCOTTE

2   woodcock

Three days before the dish is needed roast the birds, with or without the trail according to taste, in a very hot oven (220°C, 425°F, Gas Mark 7) for 10-15 minutes, according to the size of the bird. While still hot, place immediately in a small pot (just big enough to hold the birds) with a lid and baste with their juices. When cool, close the pot as tightly as possible and keep in a cool place.

After 72 hours, the woodcock will be ready to serve.

Serves 2

An alternative way of cooking woodcock that have been gutted.

1   woodcock (reserve intestines)

1 tbs   butter

1   slice streaky bacon

1   crouton

thyme or marjoram

Clean the woodcock, reserving the intestines but discarding the gizzard. Rub the bird generously with softened butter and place a slice of streaky bacon over it. Put it in an earthenware casserole, as small as possible, cover with buttered paper and then the lid. Place in a hot oven (200°C, 400°F, Gas Mark 6) and cook for about 20 minutes.

Fry a crouton and, if desired, spread with a paste made from the mashed intestines, a little butter and a small pinch of thyme or marjoram.

Place this under the bird just before serving.

Serves 1

SALMIS OF WOODCOCK

2	woodcock (reserve liver and intestines)
4	chicken livers
50ml (2fl oz)	strong stock or tinned consommé
100ml (4fl oz)	good red wine
	beurre manié
	bouquet garni of slice of onion,
	3 sprigs parsley and 1 bay leaf
½	clove garlic, crushed
6	peppercorns
1 tbs	butter
	juice of ½ lemon
	croutons
1 tbs	cream or crème fraîche – optional

Gut the woodcock, reserving the liver and intestines, and roast them in a hot oven (200°C, 400°F, Gas Mark 6) for 20 minutes. Cut in half and keep warm. Mash the intestines, livers and chicken livers into a paste and put through a fine sieve or purée in a liquidizer. Put the paste into a pan and thin with the stock and red wine. Then add a walnut-sized piece of beurre manié, stirring all the time, and add the bouquet garni, garlic and peppercorns. Simmer this very gently for 15 minutes. Remove the bouquet garni, stir in the butter, add the lemon juice to taste and add a spoonful of cream or crème fraîche to the sauce, if using. Pour the sauce over the woodcock and surround with croutons fried in butter.

Serves 2

ROAST SNIPE

1	snipe
1-2 tbs	butter
1	slice streaky bacon
1	crouton of bread
¼	lemon

If the bird is oven ready, put a knob of butter inside. If not, leave the entrails inside, but remove the gizzard. The head should be left on but skinned, then turned back and the long beak used as a skewer.

Brush the bird well with melted butter and put the slice of streaky bacon over the breast. Roast in a very hot oven (220°C, 425°F, Gas Mark 7) for 10-15 minutes, according to taste. When cooked, serve on a crouton of bread fried in butter.

Either take out the entrails, mash them and spread them on the crouton, or make a paste of sautéed chicken livers and a little butter and spread on the crouton.

Serve with a quarter of lemon and pan gravy.

Serves 1

GRILLED SNIPE

Snipe are so small that they can be grilled very quickly instead of roasting.

1	snipe
1 tbs	melted butter
1	slice streaky bacon
1	large crouton
¼	lemon

Heat the grill. Brush the bird well with melted butter, place the streaky bacon over each breast and place under a medium hot grill. Cook for about 10-15 minutes, turning and basting all the time. Serve on a crouton with a quarter of a lemon and gravy made from the pan juices.

Serves 1

WOODCOCK & SNIPE97

PIGEON

While it is not classed as game, the wild woodpigeon makes excellent eating. Large numbers are shot in this country, generally by farmers in a bid to control this "pest" from wreaking havoc on their crops. There is no close season for pigeons, but as they are more plump and fat when they have been living off the farmers' fields, they are probably best between May and October. They freeze well and are widely available from supermarkets, gamedealers and butchers.

A young pigeon has softer, pinker legs than an older bird and a round plump breast. A pigeon does not need to be hung, though the crops should be emptied out as soon as possible, particularly if the birds have been feeding on rape which can give a bitter taste to the meat.

To save the trouble of plucking and drawing, many people use the breasts only – see page 270 for preparation details.

All recipes are for oven-ready birds – one bird is usually required for each serving.

Wine recommendation

Pigeon almost falls between two stools. Freshly shot, plucked and dressed, this bird can be quite delicate and you can almost get away with a full-bodied Cru Beaujolais such as Morgon or Fleurie.

Failing that, a high quality estate Côte du Rhône would do as well. For the pigeon in chocolate sauce, indulge yourself with one of the wonderful Banyuls or Maury fortified wines from the deep south-west of France. These are among the very few wines that can cope with chocolate.

ROAST PIGEON

Only very young plump pigeons are worth roasting.

1 tbs	chopped parsley or mixed herbs
100g (4oz)	softened butter
	salt and pepper
4	young pigeons
8	slices of pork fat or streaky bacon
	flour
4	croutons
	watercress
	French dressing
	Espagnole sauce – see page 239

Mix the parsley or herbs with half the butter, add some salt and pepper and put a lump in each bird. Truss and cover the birds closely with pork fat or bacon. Place in a hot oven (200°C, 400°F, Gas Mark 6) for 20-25 minutes, basting frequently with the remaining butter. Shortly before serving, remove the fat from the birds, sprinkle with flour and allow to brown.

Serve each pigeon on a crouton of fried bread with a watercress and French dressing salad and Espagnole sauce.

Serves 4

STIR-FRIED PIGEON WITH CHORIZO
Prue Leith

8	pigeon breasts, skinned
2 tbs	grapeseed oil
100g(4oz)	chorizo, thinly sliced
5 tbs	dark soy sauce
	pepper

Cut the pigeon breasts into strips and set aside. Heat the oil in a frying-pan, add the chorizo and fry over a brisk heat until crisp. Remove with a slotted spoon and keep warm. Season the pigeon with the soy sauce and pepper. Add to the pan and stir-fry for 1-2 minutes. Return the chorizo to the pan and toss together. Pile onto a warmed serving dish.

Serves 4

PIGEONS IN CIDER

4	pigeons
2	onions, sliced
275ml (½ pint)	cider (or beer)
	bouquet garni
	pinch of mace
275ml (½ pint)	stock
	beurre manié
	juice of ½ lemon

Place the pigeons close together in a casserole and cover them with sliced onions. Pour over the cider or beer, then add the bouquet garni, mace and stock. Place in a moderately slow oven (170°C, 325°F, Gas Mark 3) for about 2 hours until tender. Remove the pigeons and keep warm. Remove the bouquet garni and thicken the gravy with beurre manié, add lemon juice to taste, pour over the birds and serve.

Serves 4

PIGEON BREASTS
STUFFED WITH CREAM CHEESE
Prue Coats

8	**pigeon breasts**
	(retain the carcasses for stock)
8 tsp	**cream cheese with herbs and garlic,**
	such as Boursin
2	**eggs beaten with 2tbs milk**
	plain flour for dredging
100-150g (4-5oz)	**fresh breadcrumbs**
100g (4oz)	**unsalted butter for frying**

Insert a sharp knife along the side of each breast and make as big a pocket as possible. Take a teaspoon of the cheese and insert with a rounded knife, spreading as evenly as possible. Dredge with flour. Dip the floured breasts in the egg and milk mixture and then coat with the breadcrumbs. Do this a second time just along the opening of the pocket to ensure that the cheese does not escape during cooking. Put the stuffed breasts in the fridge for at least half an hour, so the cream cheese is firm.

To cook, heat the butter in a thick frying-pan until it begins to foam. Drop in the breasts and cook for no more than three minutes on each side. The meat should be faintly pink and tender.

Serves 4

ORANGE AND MARSALA PIGEON

4	pigeons
4	oranges or tangerines
4	rashers bacon
2 tbs	lard or oil
1	medium onion
2	shallots
225g (8oz)	button mushrooms
I tbs	flour
	salt and pepper
1 tsp	mixed herbs
150ml (¼ pint)	Marsala or sherry

Stuff the pigeons with the whole oranges or tangerines and tie the bacon over the breast. Melt the lard or oil in a large frying-pan, brown the birds and remove to a casserole. Chop the onion and shallots finely and fry gently in the fat until soft but not coloured. Now add the mushrooms and cook for a few minutes, shaking the pan. Sprinkle in the flour, salt, ground black pepper and mixed herbs, and gradually pour in the Marsala or sherry, stirring all the time. Pour the sauce over the pigeons, cover the casserole tightly, and put in a preheated moderately hot oven (190°C, 375°F, Gas Mark 5) for about 1-1½ hours.

Serves 4

PIGEON À LA DUCK

4	pigeons
570ml (1 pint)	stock
1	onion, quartered
	pinch of mixed herbs
	peppercorns
1	bay leaf

For the sauce:

1 tbs	brown sugar
	grated peel and juice of 1 orange
225g (8oz)	sliced mushrooms, fried in butter
450ml (¾ pint)	liquid from the boiled pigeons
	(add more if necessary)
70ml (2½fl oz)	sherry, brandy or port
	beurre manié

Boil and simmer the whole pigeons in the stock, together with the onion, herbs, peppercorns and bay leaf, for 40 minutes; allow to cool in the juice.

Heat all the sauce ingredients together, stirring in a little beurre manié to thicken as necessary.

Adjust the seasoning to taste.

Remove the breasts from the pigeons, slice thinly, place in a serving dish and cover with sauce.

Serves 4

CASSEROLE OF PIGEON WITH RICE

4	young pigeons
2 tbs	olive oil
	salt and pepper
2	cloves garlic, finely chopped
2	onions, finely chopped
1	green pepper, thinly sliced
100ml (4fl oz)	white wine or water
275g (10oz)	long grain rice
50g (2oz)	pine nuts
100g (4oz)	mushrooms, sliced
1	red pepper, deseeded and sliced
2 tsp	paprika
570ml (1 pint)	stock

Heat the olive oil in a casserole and brown the pigeons well on all sides. Season with salt and pepper to taste, then add the garlic, onions, green pepper and the wine or water. Cover the casserole and place in a preheated moderate oven (180°C, 350°F, Gas Mark 4) for 20 minutes (if older pigeons are used, this may take up to an hour).

Coat the rice very lightly in a little oil. Add this to the casserole after the birds have had the first cooking, together with the pine nuts, mushrooms, red pepper and paprika. Cover with the stock, replace the casserole in the oven and cook, uncovered, until the rice is tender and the liquid is entirely absorbed – about 15-20 minutes. More liquid may be added if necessary.

The pigeons may be cut in half for this dish if desired.

Serves 4

QUICK-FRIED PIGEON

4   pigeon breasts

     butter for frying

     selection of salad leaves

For the dressing:

150ml (¼ pint)   olive oil

3 tbs   lemon juice

½   small onion, finely chopped

1 tbs   chilli sauce

1tsp   sugar

     salt and pepper to taste

Melt the butter and when it is foaming fry the pigeon breasts for about 3 minutes on each side. Put to one side and keep warm. Combine all the ingredients for the dressing and blend in a food processor or liquidizer until smooth.

Slice the pigeon breasts across the grain, place on top of a selection of salad leaves and drizzle over the dressing. Serves 2

PIGEON AND TOMATO CASSEROLE

4   pigeons

2 tbs   olive oil

1   onion, chopped

1   clove garlic, crushed

2   sticks celery, chopped

1   bay leaf

     a pinch of thyme and basil or

     a shake of Italian herbs

400g (14oz)   tin tomatoes

1 tsp   sugar

     salt and pepper

Heat the oil in a casserole and brown the pigeons. Remove and keep warm. Lightly brown the onion, garlic, celery and herbs in the oil. Add the tomatoes, sugar, salt and pepper to taste and stir well. Replace the pigeons in the sauce, baste well and cover tightly. Cook in a moderate oven (180°C, 350°F, Gas Mark 4) until the birds are tender, about 1-1½ hours,
Serves 4

If using the breasts only, cut into cubes and use as a pasta sauce.

PIGEONS EN COCOTTE

25g (1oz)	butter
4	pigeons
100g (4oz)	lardons
1	onion, finely chopped
100g (4oz)	mushrooms, sliced
1 tbs	flour
275ml (½ pint)	chicken stock
150ml (¼ pint)	white wine
	seasoning

Heat the butter and brown the pigeons slowly. Remove the pigeons and brown the lardons and onions; remove and quickly brown the mushrooms. Remove the mushrooms and shake in some flour, blend and gradually add the stock and wine. Season to taste. Return the pigeons, lardons, onions and mushrooms to the pan, spoon over the sauce, bring to boiling point, cover tightly, and cook in a moderately slow oven (170°C, 325°F, Gas Mark 3) for about 2 hours.

2 cooking apples and 150ml (¼ pint) cider can be substituted for the mushrooms and wine. Serves 4

PIGEON BREASTS WITH CABBAGE

1	medium-sized hard cabbage
10-12	pigeon breasts
10-12	slices streaky bacon
25g (1oz)	butter or bacon fat
1	onion, sliced
2	carrots, sliced
	several crushed juniper berries
	salt and pepper
	a scrape of nutmeg
450 ml (¾ pint)	stock

Cut the cabbage into fine slices, removing the hard core, and parboil in boiling salted water for 7 minutes. Drain thoroughly and press out all the water. Wrap each breast in a slice of streaky bacon and secure with a wooden toothpick. Brown the breasts in the butter or bacon fat, remove and very lightly brown the onion. Put a layer of cabbage in a deep casserole, lay the breasts on top, then the onion, carrots, juniper berries, salt, pepper and nutmeg. Cover with the remaining cabbage and pour in the stock to about halfway up. Cover with greaseproof paper and then a tight-fitting lid. Cook in a cool oven (140°C, 275°F, Gas Mark 1) for about 3 hours. Reduce the gravy or thicken with a little cornflour mixed with water, as necessary.

Serves 6

SPANISH PIGEON
IN CHOCOLATE SAUCE

Jane Grigson

4	pigeons
1	large onion, sliced
4 tbs	olive oil
150ml (¼ pint)	dry white wine
900ml (1½ pints)	chicken stock, lightly seasoned
16-24	button onions
100g (4oz)	butter
2 tsp	sugar
1 tbs	flour
2 tsp	grated plain, dark chocolate
1	lemon, cut into quarters

Brown the pigeons and sliced onion in the oil, then put them into a casserole, breast-side down. Pour in the white wine and enough chicken stock to cover the birds. Bring to the boil and simmer for 1½-2 hours until the pigeons are cooked.

An hour before the pigeons are ready, prepare the glazed onions: place enough button onions to make a single layer in a large, heavy saucepan and cover with water. Add 50g (2oz) of the butter and the sugar.

Boil hard so that the liquid evaporates to a golden brown glaze. Keep a careful eye on the onions towards the end of the cooking as they must not burn. Shake the pan gently so that they are coated in the caramel.

When the birds are almost done, that is when the legs move loosely and the meat begins to part from the breastbone, remove 570ml (1 pint) of stock from the casserole. Reduce it by boiling to just over half (this concentrates the flavour which is why only lightly seasoned chicken stock is used). Skim off the fat and foam as it rises. Mix the remaining butter with the flour to make beurre manié and add it in small pieces to the reduced stock, which should now be kept at simmer point. When the sauce has thickened, correct the seasoning and stir in the chocolate gradually, to taste.

Arrange the cooked pigeons on a warm serving dish, with the glazed onions round them. Pour a little of the sauce over the birds and put the rest into a sauce-boat. Arrange the lemon wedges among the onions.

Serves 4

STIR-FRIED PIGEON
Prue Coats

8	pigeon breasts
	butter for frying
4oz (100g)	mushrooms (preferably oyster mushrooms)
1 tsp	good quality redcurrant jelly
2-3	good shakes of soy sauce
1	shake of Worcestershire sauce
	salt and pepper
150ml (¼ pint)	single cream or half cream
	and half Greek yoghurt

Cut the pigeon breasts into thin strips lengthways. Heat the butter in a wok or large frying-pan until foaming and cook the meat for a few seconds, stirring all the time. Add all the other ingredients, except the cream, cook for a few seconds more then add the cream. The meat should be a little pink inside.

Serve with rice or on thick slices of buttered toast.

Serves 2-4

PIGIEBURGERS

2	pigeon breasts
50-75g (2-3oz)	belly pork
½	small onion
	a few fresh herbs
	a little olive oil
	salt and pepper

Coarsely mince the pigeon breasts and belly pork and mix in the finely chopped onion and chopped herbs – alternatively pass the first four ingredients through the mincer. Add a little oil and season well. Mix thoroughly. Form into burgers and fry in a little olive oil until just cooked – about 2-3 minutes each side.

Serve in a bap with tomato salsa (see page 253).

Makes 2 burgers

This works well with pheasant breasts too.

WILD DUCK

The best known of the wild duck, and the most commonly eaten, is the mallard. Wigeon and teal may also end up in the game larder and they, too, make very good eating. Wild duck sometimes have a fishy flavour, owing to the diet of the bird; also if the gut has been punctured, the flavour may not be so good. To rectify this, place an onion or potato inside its cavity with a teaspoon of salt. Place the bird in a pan with 5mm (¼in) boiling water and bake in a moderate oven (180°C, 350°F, Gas Mark 4), basting frequently, for 10 minutes. Drain the bird and remove the onion or potato. If buying oven-ready duck from a gamedealer or poulterer, this should not be necessary.

It is not easy to tell the age of a wild duck, though the webbing of the feet of a young duck can usually be torn quite easily and the feet are pinker and the bills brighter than in older birds. A wild duck does not need prolonged hanging; one to two days is all that is required otherwise it may become rancid. Unlike thier domestic cousin, wild duck are virtually fat free so extra fat needs to be used in the cooking to prevent the meat from becoming dry. Roast wild duck is generally served pink and should never be overcooked as it will dry out. All the recipes are for oven-ready mallard-sized duck unless otherwise stated. One bird generally feeds two to three people. For preparation details, see page 270.

Wine recommendation

The classic variety to serve with duck is Pinot Noir. The general rule of thumb is the richer the sauce the heavier the style of Pinot Noir. Start with wines from Burgundy's Côte-de-Beaune (the lightest) such as Chorey-les-Beaune, Volnay and red Chassagne-Montrachet and move up to heavier styles such as Gevrey-Chambertin and Nuits-St-Georges. Quality varies in Burgundy from producer to producer and vintage to vintage, so it is best to seek advice from your merchant prior to making a purchase. The exception to this rule is wild teal, which goes perfectly with Grenache-dominated wines of the southern Rhône, especially a light Châteauneuf-du-Pape or a good Gigondas. Duck in yoghurt with chilli requires a white Alsatian, preferably Riesling or Pinot Gris rather than Gewurztraminer. The crisp, dry and alluring style of a classic Alsace Riesling will stand up very well to the mixed spices.

ROAST WILD MALLARD

If a crisp skin is desired, pour a kettle of boiling water over the oven-ready bird and allow to cool.

Pat dry and leave for 2-3 hours. When ready to cook the bird, rub with oil and a sprinkling of salt. Roast, uncovered, basting two or three times.

1	wild duck
1	knob of seasoned butter
	softened butter
1	orange – or apple, onion or game stuffing if preferred
	a little red wine, port or orange juice

To serve: orange and watercress salad
            (see page 268)
            sauce Bigarade (see page 239)

Place the orange and a knob of seasoned butter inside the cavity and truss. Smear the breasts with softened butter, place in a very hot oven (230°C, 450°F, Gas Mark 8), and pour over red wine, port, or orange juice. Baste frequently. How long to cook wild duck is a matter of personal taste – usually between 20 and 30 minutes is about right. Do not overcook them.

Add a little more wine, orange juice or redcurrant jelly to the juices, or serve with Sauce Bigarade and Orange and watercress salad.

Serves 2-3

Teal can be roasted in a similar way but only fill the cavity with seasoned butter – any other stuffing seems to overpower its flavour. Baste frequently with butter, dust slightly with flour just as it is ready and baste again. It will probably take 12-20 minutes.

DUCK WITH APPLES AND CIDER

1	medium-sized duck
	salt
275ml (½ pint)	dry cider
150ml (¼ pint)	cream
2 tbs	water
For the stuffing:	
75g (3oz)	butter
100g (4oz)	white fresh breadcrumbs
450g (1lb)	cooking apples skinned, cored and diced
	salt and pepper
2 tsp	sugar
	ground cinnamon

Rub salt into the duck skin. Make the stuffing by melting the butter in a frying-pan, add the breadcrumbs and fry until golden brown. Add the apples, cover, and cook until soft – about 15 minutes. Season to taste with salt, pepper, sugar and cinnamon. When cool, stuff the duck and close the tail end with a skewer. Place in roasting tin with 2 tbs water and cook in a moderate oven (180°C, 350°F, Gas Mark 4) for 20 minutes per 450g (1lb).

About 15 minutes before the end of the cooking time, remove the duck from the oven, drain off the fat, and pour the cider over the duck and replace in the oven. When cooked, remove the duck from the roasting-tin and keep warm; simmer the cider until it is reduced by half.

Cut the duck into four portions and arrange on a serving dish. Put the stuffing in a small basin. Add the cream to the gravy and strain over the duck.

Serves 2-3

CHINESE GINGERED DUCK

4	duck breasts, thinly sliced
50g (2oz)	fresh ginger, peeled and
	cut into fine strips
2 tbs	oil
50g (2oz)	flaked almonds
2	cloves garlic, crushed
2 tbs	soy sauce
2 tbs	dry sherry
4	spring onions, finely shredded

Mix the duck with the ginger and leave, covered, for half an hour. Heat the oil in a wok or large frying-pan and cook the almonds until golden brown. Transfer them to a plate with a slotted spoon. Add the garlic to the pan, then the duck and the ginger, and stir-fry for about 5 minutes or until the duck is just cooked.

Add all the other ingredients, except the almonds, and cook over a high heat for a few seconds. Sprinkle the almonds on top and serve with egg noodles, beansprouts and fine green beans.

Serves 4-6

WILD DUCK WITH CHERRIES

2	wild duck
	salt and pepper
50g (2oz)	butter
1 tin	stoned black cherries
275ml (½ pint)	port
1 tsp	cornflour

Cut the duck in half. Sprinkle with salt and pepper and brown in butter rather slowly so they become golden all over. Drain off the butter and add the juice from a tin of stoned cherries and the port.

Cover and simmer for 1½ hours or until the birds are tender. Remove the birds to a hot platter, cover and keep warm. Skim the fat from the juices, then add the cornflour mixed with a little water. Bring to the boil, stirring all the time, and simmer until thickened. Add the cherries and simmer until they are heated through.

Serves 4-6

WILD DUCK MAISON

2	wild duck, cut into joints
25g (1oz)	butter
2 tbs	oil
4 tbs	Marsala
2 tbs	tomato purée
2 tbs	flour
450ml (¾ pint)	chicken stock
	salt and pepper
1	bay leaf
5-6	mushrooms
1	red pepper, diced
½	green pepper, diced
1 tsp	orange rind,
	finely chopped
1	orange, segmented
3	tomatoes, skinned and sliced

Brown the duck joints all over in half the butter and oil, pour over the Marsala, then remove the duck and add tomato purée and flour; blend well and pour on the chicken stock. Allow to come to the boil, put back the joints, season with salt and pepper, add a bay leaf and allow to simmer gently until tender, about 45 minutes.

Meanwhile, slice the mushrooms and sauté them in the remaining butter, add the red and green peppers, orange rind, orange segments and tomato slices; cook together very gently. Remove the duck joints from their gravy and thicken if necessary.

Add the orange mixture and pour over the ducks on a warm platter.

Serves 4-6

SALMIS OF WILD DUCK

175g (6oz)	lardons
75g (3oz)	butter
1	onion, finely chopped
1	bouquet garni
2	wild duck
25g (1oz)	flour
450ml (¾ pint)	good stock (game or chicken)
275ml (½ pint)	red wine
	olives – optional

Fry the lardons until crisp (using a little fat if necessary), put half to one side and transfer the rest to a roasting tin. Add half the butter, the onion, bouquet garni and the duck and roast for 20 minutes in a moderately slow oven (170°C, 325°F, Gas Mark 3), basting occasionally. Pour off the liquid, skim off the fat and retain the juices. Carve the meat from the duck and keep warm. In another saucepan, melt the rest of the butter and fry the flour until it turns brown, then add the stock and red wine, mix until smooth, bring to the boil and simmer on the top of the oven for 30 minutes or more.

Add the juices from the duck meat.

Place the duck meat in a casserole with the reserved bacon and a few olives if using. Pour the sauce over the meat and simmer for 15 minutes or until tender.

Serves 4-6

MARINATED WILD DUCK

2	wild duck
1 tbs	flour
3 tbs	olive oil
1	clove garlic, crushed
225g (8oz)	mushrooms, sliced
1 tsp	cornflour
	salt and pepper

For the marinade:

100ml (4fl oz)	brandy
150ml (¼ pint)	red wine
2	onions, sliced
1 tbs	chopped parsley
½ tsp	thyme
1	bay leaf
¼ tsp	allspice

Combine all the ingredients for the marinade, cut the duck in half and place them in a bowl with the marinade. Leave for at least 6 hours or preferably overnight, turning several times. Dry the duck, sprinkle with flour and brown in olive oil.

Transfer to a casserole, strain the marinade over and add the garlic. Bring to a simmer and add the mushrooms. Cover, and simmer slowly for 1½ hours or until the duck meat is tender.

Thicken the gravy with cornflour mixed with water.

Season to taste.

Serves 4-6

WILD DUCK
WITH ONIONS AND TURNIPS

3 tbs	butter
1 tbs	oil
2	wild duck
275ml (½ pint)	stock
150ml (¼ pint)	white wine
	bouquet garni consisting of celery, parsley, bay leaf and thyme
	salt and pepper
18	button onions
	a little sugar
450g (1lb)	baby turnips or large turnips cut into 2.5cm (1in) cubes

Melt 1 tbs of the butter and the oil in a casserole. Slowly brown the duck all over, adding more fat if necessary. Add the stock, wine, bouquet garni, salt and pepper to the casserole, and bring to a simmer. Cook in a moderate oven (180°C, 350°F, Gas Mark 4) for 45 minutes.

Melt the remaining butter in a pan, add the onions, sprinkle with a little sugar and cook until golden. Remove. Add the turnips and cook until golden. Add both of these to the casserole and cook for a further 45 minutes. Remove the duck, cut in half or in serving pieces, place on a platter and surround with the vegetables. Skim the fat from the gravy, thicken slightly if necessary and pour over the meat.

Serves 4-6

DUCK IN YOGHURT

1	wild duck, cut into serving pieces
1	onion, chopped
2 tbs	oil
1	large tomato, chopped
⅛ tsp	coriander seeds
1 tsp	ground cumin
1 tsp	chilli powder
1 tsp	turmeric
	salt to taste
570ml (1 pint)	plain yoghurt
1	clove garlic and 1cm (½ in) fresh ginger mashed together
275ml (½ pint)	water

Brown the duck and onion in the oil. Add the tomato, spices and yoghurt. Fry for a few minutes and then add the garlic and ginger mixture and stir in the water. Cook, uncovered, for 5 minutes, then cover and simmer for 2 hours. Add more water if needed. Serve with pilau rice.

Serves 2-3

DUCK AND PASTA SALAD

1	wild duck, roasted
1	orange
4-5	chicory leaves, chopped
6-8oz	cooked pasta shapes, such as fusilli
	a little lemon thyme, chopped

For the dressing:

150ml (¼ pint)	olive oil
1 tbs	wine vinegar
1-2 tbs	lemon juice
1	clove garlic, crushed
	salt and pepper
To serve:	a selection of leaves

When the roast duck has cooled, take off the meat and cut into bite-size chunks. Mix with the cooked pasta. Peel the orange and cut out segments, removing skin and pith, and stir into the salad with the chopped chicory leaves.

Mix the dressing ingredients together and pour over the salad. Mix well and serve with a selection of leaves.

Serves 2-3

LAZY DUCK WITH ORANGE

2 tbs	butter
	marjoram
	parsley
½	orange
1	wild duck
2 tbs	thick cut marmalade
	juice of 2 oranges
	a little stock or water
	salt and pepper
	a squeeze of lemon

Place half of the butter, a little marjoram and parsley, and half an orange inside the duck. Spread the duck with the remaining butter and then the marmalade, according to taste. Squeeze the juice of 2 oranges into the bottom of the pan and add a little water or stock. Cover loosely with foil and place in a moderate oven (180°C, 350°F, Gas Mark 4). Baste frequently, adding more juice, water or stock if necessary, until the bird is cooked but still pink – about ½-¾ hour. If it is an older bird cook, covered, in a casserole at a lower heat for longer.

Ten minutes before the bird is ready, remove the foil, but carry on basting. When the bird is cooked, remove, keep warm, and scrape up all the juices from the pan. Season with salt, pepper and a squeeze of lemon to taste. Thicken if necessary with a little cornflour mixed with water.

Serves 2-3

ROAST DUCK WITH CREAM CHEESE

For a crisp skin, see tip on page 114.

1	wild duck
2-3 tbs	unsalted cream cheese
	a little parsley, thyme, basil or marjoram
1 tbs	softened butter
2-3 strips	streaky bacon

Place the cream cheese, with some herbs, inside the cavity. Spread the bird with the softened butter and cover with the strips of streaky bacon.

Roast in a very hot oven (220°C, 425°F, Gas Mark 7) for 25-30 minutes – according to personal preference. The cream cheese should produce enough gravy to serve with the duck.

Serves 2-3

WHISKY DUCK

1	wild duck
2 tbs	green peppercorns
25g (1oz)	butter
2 tbs	whisky (or brandy)

Place the peppercorns and half the butter inside the bird; use the rest of the butter to rub over the outside of the bird. Place on one side in a casserole and pour over the whisky or brandy. Cover well and place in a moderate oven (180°C, 350°F, Gas Mark 4) for 1-1¼ hours.

Turn the bird halfway through the cooking time.

Ten minutes before it is cooked, remove the cover and turn the bird breast-side up in order to brown evenly. Add a few more peppercorns to the juices if desired.

Serves 2-3

WILD GOOSE

There are four species of wild goose on the quarry list in Britain: the Canada is the largest, being about twice the size of the other three – the greylag, pink-footed and white-fronted. Opinion varies as to which is the best to eat and each has its own unique flavour. The meat can have a strong taste which lends itself very well to game pies and pâtés.

As with wild duck, there is little fat on a wild goose so much basting is called for when roasting. It is illegal to sell wild geese in Britain, but a friendly farmer may be willing to hand over one or two if he has had success with the gun. For those who find themselves with a glut of wild geese it is easier, though more extravagant, to use the breasts only and either discard the rest of the bird or keep it to make stock.

Geese can be hung for anything up to three weeks, according to personal preference. Ageing geese is never easy and gets increasingly harder as the season progresses so unless it is clearly a young goose, it is advisable to slow roast it otherwise the meat will be very tough.

For preparation details, see page 270.

A Canada goose will serve 6-8 people, with the other three species serving about 2-4 according to size.

Wine recommendation

As wild goose always has much less fat than a domestic bird, a traditional Claret, preferably a Pomerol with some bottle age, would be perfect, or a light Pinot Noir, preferably a Burgundy Côte-de-Beaune. Alternatively, try a big white wine such as a full-bodied Meursault, Chassagne-Montrachet or Puligny-Montrachet. To be really different, and for something that you can enjoy with your cheese afterwards, try an Alsace Riesling Grand Cru.

ROAST GOOSE

1	goose
50g (2oz)	softened butter
	orange juice, wine or stock for basting

For the stuffing:

50-75g (2-3oz)	butter
1	large onion, chopped
1	large apple, cored, peeled and sliced
2 tsp	dried sage, thyme or small
	handful of fresh herbs
	grated rind and juice of ½ lemon
4-6	pickled walnuts, coarsely
	chopped – optional
225g (8oz)	breadcrumbs
1	egg, beaten lightly
	salt and pepper

To make the stuffing, melt the butter and lightly fry the onion; add all the remaining stuffing ingredients. As the goose has no fat of its own, the stuffing should be full of butter, though not saturated.

Truss the goose well, getting the legs and wings in as close as possible to the body. Rub the bird generously with softened butter. Roast, breast down, turning it from one side to the other occasionally or roast on a trivet in a very hot oven (230°C, 450°F, Gas Mark 8) for about 10 minutes, then turn down the heat to (170°C, 325°F, Gas Mark 3) and cook until the juices run clear, about 1-1¼ hours. Baste frequently, adding orange juice, wine or stock to the basting liquid.

Place the goose on a platter, skim the fat from the juices and reduce to thicken very slightly. Alternatively serve with sauce Bigarade (see page 239) or prune sauce (see page 240).

CASSEROLED WILD GOOSE

Use a heavy casserole (such as Le Creuset) in which the bird fits as neatly as possible. If cooking two birds, use two casseroles.

1	onion, halved
1	stick celery
1	wild goose
1 tbs	oil
1 tbs	butter
275ml (½ pint)	red wine (or a mixture of red wine and stock)
1	bay leaf
	black pepper
1-2	sprigs thyme
1 tbs	redcurrant jelly
	cornflour

Place the onion and celery inside the bird and truss the legs together well.

Brown the bird in a mixture of oil and butter in the casserole, leave the bird breast down, pour over the red wine or wine and stock, then put in the bay leaf, a couple of turns of the pepper-grinder and a sprig of thyme. Bring to a simmer and place in a moderately slow oven (170°C, 325°F, Gas Mark 3) for about 2 hours, basting occasionally.

When the bird is cooked, strain off the juices. Melt the redcurrant jelly in the juices and thicken slightly with a little cornflour mixed with water.

Add sautéed onions or mushrooms to the juices while the bird is cooking or add sour cream to the sauce at the end of the cooking time.

GOOSE AND AVOCADO SALAD

350g (12oz)	cold cooked goose
1	large ripe avocado
2	large oranges
2 tbs	olive oil
2 tbs	lemon juice
	salt and pepper
	a few croutons – optional

Peel the avocado, remove the stone and slice thinly. Place in a large serving bowl. Using a sharp knife, peel off the skin and pith from the oranges. Hold over the serving bowl and cut out segments from the fruit, discarding skin and pips. Combine the oil and lemon juice and pour over the avocado and oranges, mixing lightly.

Season the goose meat with salt and pepper and combine with the fruit mixture. Scatter with croutons, if using.

Serves 3-4

BREASTS OF GOOSE DONE ANYHOW

For the marinade:	2 tbs	lemon juice
	3-4 tbs	olive oil
		a pinch of mixed herbs
	6-8	peppercorns, crushed
	2	wild goose breasts
		seasoned flour
		butter for frying
	1	onion, peeled and chopped
	1	small tin tomatoes
150ml (¼ pint)		red wine
		stock to cover

Combine the marinade and pour over the breasts (if the breasts are thick, cut the meat on the bias into serving slices). Leave for several hours, remove from the marinade, dry and toss in seasoned flour. Melt the butter and brown the meat; add the onion and fry gently for a few minutes, then add the tomatoes, red wine and enough stock to cover. Simmer for about an hour. If using a young goose, sauté the meat with onion and green pepper, make a stroganoff with onion and cream, or stir-fry.

Serves 2-3

BREADED WILD GOOSE

A very young fat goose is needed for this recipe.

For the stuffing:

	liver of goose
1	slice of onion
½	clove garlic, mashed
	a little parsley
	a little thyme
5-6	juniper berries, crushed
25g (1oz)	butter

1	wild goose
50g (2oz)	butter
1 tsp	prepared mustard
100g (4oz)	fine breadcrumbs

Mix the stuffing ingredients together and place inside the goose, sew up the cavity and truss. Rub the goose all over thickly with the 50g (2oz) of butter. Place, breast-down, on a trivet and roast for 1 hour in a moderately hot oven (190°C, 375°F, Gas Mark 5), basting frequently. About 10 minutes before the bird is done, remove it from the oven. Add the mustard to the pan juices and stir. Take the bird off the trivet, place in the pan on its back and sprinkle some breadcrumbs over it, baste it well again and sprinkle more crumbs until it is entirely covered.

Finish roasting until the crumbs are golden brown.

Serve with brown mustard sauce (see page 242) or apple sauce (see page 62).

WILD GOOSE WITH GREEN PEPPER SAUCE

1 **wild goose**

fatty streaky bacon

   (enough to cover the breast)

For the stock:

   giblets from the bird

1 **onion, sliced**

1 **carrot, sliced**

   salt and pepper

   thyme

1 **bay leaf**

1 **onion, halved**

1 **carrot**

   a little Cognac

   a few shakes of green

     pepper Tabasco sauce

Cover the breast with streaky bacon and roast in a hot oven (200°C, 400°F, Gas Mark 6) for 20-30 minutes. Meanwhile, make a stock by simmering the giblets, onion and carrot in hot water. Take the bird out of the oven and remove the bacon. Season with salt and pepper and put the thyme, bay leaf, onion and carrot inside.

Put it back in the roasting tin, breast down, and pour over the strained stock and a little Cognac, and cover with foil.

Turn the oven right down to (150°C, 300°F, Gas Mark 2) and braise the goose very slowly for 2½-3 hours, basting with the juices and turning it several times.

For the last 30 minutes turn the goose on its back and turn up the heat to (180°C, 350°F, Gas Mark 4).

Carve the meat, which should be quite tender and very dark brown all over, and transfer to a warm serving dish. Strain the pan juices into a saucepan and add the green pepper Tabasco; let it reduce a little, then pour over the meat.

WILD GOOSE SHEPHERD'S PIE

450g (1lb)	wild goose breasts
1	onion, chopped
100ml (4fl oz)	olive oil
1	small tin of tomatoes
	stock or red wine
	salt and pepper
	carrots, diced – optional
	celery, chopped – optional
	turnip, diced – optional
900g (2lb)	mashed potatoes
1 tbs	butter

Mince the goose breasts fairly coarsely. Chop the onion and brown it slowly in the olive oil, add the mince and brown all over. Add the tinned tomatoes and enough stock or red wine to just cover the meat. Cover and simmer for an hour or two, depending on the age of the bird, adding the vegetables, if using, about halfway through the cooking time.

Put the mince in a pie dish and add a little more liquid if it has cooked away. Cover with very creamy mashed potatoes, dot the top with butter and bake in a moderately hot oven (190°C, 375°F, Gas Mark 5) for 20 minutes.

This can take a thicker layer of potatoes than the usual shepherd's pie as the goose meat is quite rich.

Serves 4

RABBIT

Rabbit is widely available throughout the year and has no close season. The meat is very low in fat and can be used in a wide variety of recipes and is especially good when casseroled. Younger rabbits, aged between three and four months, make the best eating.

There is some prejudice against eating rabbit no doubt stemming from the days when myxomatosis all but wiped out the rabbit population back in the 1950s. Today rabbit numbers are estimated to be in excess of 37 million and they provide an excellent source of protein. The wild rabbit has a better flavour than those bred for the table, but beware the big old buck which can have a much stronger flavour and be somewhat tough. To get rid of any strong taste, soak them in salted water for several hours,

changing the water as frequently as possible. A slice of lemon added to the water will whiten the meat. As they have little natural fat, rabbits must be well barded (covered in pork fat or bacon) and cooked with plenty of butter or oil. A rabbit improves with marinating, preferably overnight. Use white wine or lemon juice in the marinade, unless the rabbit is to be cooked in red wine. Rabbit livers are delicious; the kidneys can be eaten, too, but the gall bladder (found in a recess of the biggest lobe) must be removed to avoid a bitter taste. Rabbits can be eaten fresh or hung by the hind legs for 3-4 days, but they must be paunched – or gutted – as soon as they have been killed.

For preparation details, see page 270.

Wine recommendation

A good Chianti Classico or southern Rhône, such as Cairanne, would be perfect with rabbit. A wine with a touch of aromatic fruit to it, such as an Alsace Gewurtztraminer, would go well with the rabbit satay, but any dish with vinegar in it is almost impossible to match with wine with successful results. A better alternative is to have something completely different, such as real ale.

ROAST RABBIT   CIVET DE LAPIN

For the marinade: 3 tbs olive oil

275ml (½ pint) white or red wine

1 slice of onion

1 clove of garlic, crushed

1 bay leaf

a good squeeze of lemon juice

or 2 tbs wine vinegar

1 young rabbit

50g (2oz) softened butter

4 slices of pork fat or streaky bacon

Combine the marinade ingredients and pour over the rabbit; leave for several hours or preferably overnight. Remove and dry well. Strain the marinade. Cover the rabbit with softened butter and place some inside. Cover in pork fat or bacon, and place in a hot oven (200°C, 400°F, Gas Mark 6) for an hour, basting frequently with the butter and marinade.

Remove the rabbit from the oven and skim any excess fat from the juices. Add more wine if needed and thicken with a little beurre manié, if necessary.   Serves 4

For the marinade:

½ bottle Burgundy

1-2 carrots, sliced

1 onion, sliced

3-4 cloves of garlic

a little oil

bouquet garni of parsley,

thyme and a bay leaf

1 rabbit, jointed

butter or oil for frying

2 tbs flour

2 glasses brandy

1 tbs tomato purée

stock to cover (this can be made

using a chicken stock cube)

salt and pepper

18-20 button onions

a pinch of sugar

350g (¾lb)	lardons
350-450g (¾-1lb)	mushrooms, cut into quarters
	blood from rabbit – optional
	beurre manié – optional
To garnish:	chopped parsley and croutons

Combine the marinade ingredients. Marinate the rabbit joints for 3-4 hours, turning from time to time. Remove the rabbit, dry well and retain the marinade.

Melt the butter or oil in a large casserole. When hot, add the rabbit, turning frequently to brown all over. Add the flour and mix so that the rabbit is well coated. Pour over the brandy and ignite. Add the marinade and tomato purée, stir well and pour in enough stock to cover the meat. Season to taste, cover and cook for about 30-45 minutes slowly on the hob, or until the meat is cooked through, stirring from time to time to prevent the meat from sticking. Remove the meat to a warmed dish and cover it.

Meanwhile, cook the onions in boiling water for 5 minutes, refresh and drain. Sauté in a pan with butter, salt, pepper and a pinch of sugar until golden. Remove and add to the rabbit. In the same pan, sauté the lardons until slightly coloured, add the mushrooms and sauté for a few minutes, adding butter, salt and pepper, if necessary; add to the rabbit and keep warm.

To make the sauce, strain the liquid in which the meat has been cooked into the sauté pan and stir well. If a thicker sauce is required, add beurre manié a little at a time. If using the blood, add a little of the sauce to the blood, off the heat, then add this to the rest of the sauce on the heat stirring well.

Pour the sauce over the rabbit and reheat for a few minutes if necessary. Arrange large croutons around the dish and garnish with chopped parsley.

Serves 4

SWEET AND SOUR RABBIT
Angela Humphreys

2	young rabbits jointed
1 432g	tin pineapple pieces
6	large tomatoes, chopped
1	large green pepper,
	deseeded and chopped
1	large onion, finely chopped
1 tbs	soft brown sugar
2 tbs	white wine vinegar
2 tbs	soy sauce
	salt and pepper
1 tbs	cornflour

Soak the rabbit joints in cold water for 24 hours, then rinse thoroughly. Place all the ingredients, except the cornflour, in a large saucepan and simmer gently for 1 hour or until tender. Allow the joints to cool, remove the meat from the bones and cut the meat into small pieces.

Mix the cornflour with water, blend into the sauce and bring to the boil stirring all the time.

Return the rabbit meat to the sauce and reheat gently. Turn into a large warmed shallow dish and serve with plain rice or pasta and a variety of salads.

Serves 8

BAKED RABBIT WITH RED ONIONS, TOMATO AND TURMERIC

Prue Leith

2 tbs	olive oil
1	large rabbit, skinned and jointed
	seasoned flour
2	large red onions, sliced
2	large cloves of garlic, crushed
1 tbs	ground turmeric
275ml (½ pt)	dry white wine
450g (1lb)	ripe tomatoes, skinned and chopped
1 tbs	tomato purée
1	bay leaf
	a pinch of sugar
275ml (½ pt)	chicken stock
	salt and pepper
2 tbs	roughly chopped flat leaf parsley

Heat the oil in a large heavy-based casserole, coat the rabbit joints in the seasoned flour and pat off the excess. Gently brown the rabbit joints on all sides and transfer them to a plate.

Add the onions to the pan and cook until golden brown adding more oil if necessary. Add the garlic and turmeric and cook for 1 minute. Pour in the wine and boil rapidly stirring any sediment off the bottom of the pan until almost completely reduced. Add the tomatoes, tomato purée, bay leaf, sugar and stock, and season with salt and pepper.

Bring to the boil, return the rabbit joints to the pan, cover with a close fitting lid and cook in a moderately cool oven (160°C, 325°F, Gas Mark 3) for ¾-1 hour or until the rabbit is tender.

Lift the rabbit out of the sauce and transfer to a warmed serving dish. Bring the sauce back to the boil, reduce to a syrupy consistency, season to taste and pour over the rabbit. Sprinkle with parsley.

Serves 4

CASSEROLE OF RABBIT WITH WHITE WINE

1	rabbit cut into pieces
225g (8oz)	streaky bacon
2 tbs	seasoned flour
2	large onions, thinly sliced
75g (3oz)	butter
150ml (¼ pint)	white wine or cider
275ml (½ pint)	stock
1	clove garlic, crushed
1	bouquet garni of bay leaf, parsley and thyme
1 tbs	finely chopped parsley

Dry the rabbit well and roll in seasoned flour, then wrap each piece with slices of bacon. Secure with wooden toothpicks and brown, with the onions, in the butter. Alternatively, coarsely dice the bacon and brown with the rabbit pieces and onions. Place in a casserole with the wine or cider, stock, garlic and bouquet garni. Cover and simmer until tender, about 1½ hours. When the rabbit is cooked, remove the bouquet garni and strain off the sauce. Reduce if necessary or thicken with flour mixed with a little stock. Pour back over the rabbit and serve sprinkled with finely chopped parsley.

Variations: Add some tomato purée or 3 sliced, cored and peeled green apples when adding the wine and stock, or sauté some mushrooms and add them to the sauce.

Serves 4

GARLIC RABBIT WITH PANCETTA

RABBIT IN BEER

4	rabbit joints
	seasoned wholemeal flour
	a sprig of thyme, chopped
1	clove garlic, crushed
	butter for frying
8	slices of pancetta or smoked bacon
To serve:	a selection of leaves

Dip the rabbit joints in the seasoned wholemeal flour until well covered. Melt the butter in a large frying-pan and heat until foaming. Fry the joints, together with the thyme and garlic, until cooked through – about 15 minutes.

Meanwhile fry the pancetta or smoked bacon and serve, with the rabbit joints, on a bed of leaves.

Serves 4

1	rabbit
8-10	potatoes, peeled and sliced
3	onions, sliced
2 tbs	butter or margarine
	salt and pepper
1	bottle light beer

Cut the rabbit into serving pieces. Melt the butter in a large pan or casserole and brown the rabbit. Season with salt and pepper to taste. Take out the rabbit, then put the sliced potatoes and onions in the pan and arrange the rabbit on top. Add salt to flavour the potatoes, and pour the beer over the rabbit. Cover with a lid and let simmer slowly until the rabbit is tender, about 1-1½ hours

Serves 4

RABBIT FRICASSÉE

1	rabbit
1	onion, sliced
1	carrot, sliced
1	celery stick, sliced
4 tbs	butter
	salt and pepper
1 tbs	flour
570ml (1 pint)	boiling chicken stock
150ml (¼ pint)	white wine
1	bouquet garni
	water to cover
2	egg yolks
150ml (¼ pint)	double cream
	squeeze of lemon juice
	scrape of nutmeg
100g (4oz)	sautéed mushrooms and/or
	16 sautéed button onions

Cut the rabbit into serving pieces and dry thoroughly. Sauté the onion, carrot and celery gently in the butter until they are soft. Add the rabbit pieces and turn in butter until golden. Cover and cook very slowly for 10 minutes. Sprinkle salt, pepper and flour over the rabbit, so it is coated on all sides, and cook for a few minutes more. Pour in the boiling stock and white wine, add the bouquet garni and enough water so that the liquid covers the rabbit. Cover and simmer slowly for 45 minutes or until tender. Drain off the liquid and reduce it to about 570ml (1 pint).

Whisk the egg yolks with the double cream, add some of the hot liquid to this and then whisk it back into the remaining sauce. Heat quickly, stirring all the time. Add salt and pepper, if necessary, and lemon juice and nutmeg. Place the rabbit on a serving dish, pour over the sauce and surround with sautéed mushrooms and/or sautéed button onions.

Serves 4

RABBIT IN RED WINE

For the marinade:

150ml (¼ pint)	red wine vinegar
3 tbs	olive oil
2	large cloves garlic
1	large onion, sliced
	a few crushed juniper berries
	freshly ground black pepper
1	bay leaf
	a little marjoram and thyme – optional
1	rabbit
100g (4oz)	lardons
2 tbs	olive oil
2	onions, sliced
	salt and pepper
570ml (1 pint)	red wine
570ml (1 pint)	stock
1 tbs	cornflour
225g (8oz)	mushrooms, sautéed
1 tbs	finely chopped parsley
	croutons

Combine all the ingredients for the marinade. Cut the rabbit into pieces and marinate for a day or more in the refrigerator. Brown the lardons in olive oil, then add the onions and cook until soft. Remove. Dry the rabbit well and brown, adding more oil if necessary. Put the onion, bacon and rabbit in the casserole, and season with salt and pepper. In a separate saucepan, reduce the strained marinade until it has nearly evaporated, then add the red wine. Reduce this slightly, add the stock and pour back into the casserole. Simmer slowly on the hob or in moderate oven (180°C, 350°F, Gas Mark 4) until tender, about 1½ hours.

When the rabbit is cooked, drain off the sauce and skim off the fat, then either reduce further or thicken with a little cornflour mixed with water. Add mushrooms if using. Sprinkle with parsley and surround with croutons.

Serves 4

MARINATED RABBIT WITH APPLES

For the marinade:

1	sliced onion
1	sliced carrot
2	sprigs parsley,
1	bay leaf
	salt and pepper
	thyme
150ml (¼ pint)	white wine,
1 tbs	olive oil

1	rabbit
2 tbs	butter
3	green apples, sliced, cored
3	onions, sliced
275ml (½ pint)	cream or crème fraîche
	juice of ½ lemon

Combine all the marinade ingredients. Cut the rabbit into pieces and marinate in the refrigerator overnight. Dry the rabbit pieces and brown lightly in the butter. Remove and add the apples and onions and cook for a few minutes. Put the rabbit back into the pan and add the cream. Cover and cook very slowly on the hob for about 1½ hours or until tender. Remove the meat and keep warm.

Put the sauce through a liquidizer with the lemon juice. Reheat the sauce and pour over the rabbit.

Serves 4

RABBIT WITH MUSTARD

1	rabbit
4-5	slices streaky bacon
2 tbs	butter
2 tbs	oil
3	medium onions, chopped
1	small clove garlic, crushed
3	carrots, sliced
2 tbs	brandy
150ml (¼ pint)	dry white wine
150ml (¼ pint)	chicken stock
	a little thyme
1	bay leaf
1 tsp	English mustard
2 tsp	Dijon mustard
150ml (¼ pint)	double cream
1 tbs	finely chopped parsley

Cut a young tender rabbit into serving pieces and wrap each piece in streaky bacon, securing with wooden toothpicks. Brown these until golden in butter and oil. Remove the rabbit and brown the onions, garlic and carrots in the remaining fat. Replace the rabbit and add the brandy, dry white wine and chicken stock. Sprinkle with thyme and add the bay leaf, then cover, and cook very gently until tender – about 1 hour.

Remove the rabbit from the casserole and keep warm; discard the bay leaf.

Skim the fat from the sauce and whisk in the mustards and double cream; stir well and heat carefully. Pour over the rabbit and sprinkle with parsley.

Serves 4

RABBIT SATAY
WITH SPICY PEANUT SAUCE

Hugh Fearnley-Whittingstall

550-675g			**For the spicy peanut sauce:**	
(1¼-1½ lb)	lean rabbit meat, cubed		1	onion, finely chopped
	bamboo skewers		2	garlic cloves, crushed
For the marinade:			1 tbs	groundnut or sunflower oil
	a walnut-sized piece of fresh		½-1	fresh red or green chilli,
	ginger root, finely grated			finely chopped (to taste or use
1-3	fresh chillies (to taste), finely chopped			bottled chilli sauce)
2	garlic cloves, crushed		2-3 tbs	dark soy sauce
½	small onion, grated		1 tbs	brown sugar
2 tsp	coriander seeds, crushed		120g (4½oz)	crunchy peanut butter
2 tbs	dark soy sauce			juice of ½ lime
2 tbs	brown sugar			
	juice of ½ lime			

continued overleaf

RABBIT WITH TARRAGON

Mix all the ingredients for the marinade together in a large bowl, add the rabbit meat and leave in the fridge for at least 2 hours. Soak the bamboo skewers in cold water for at least half an hour.

For the spicy peanut sauce, gently cook the onion and garlic in the oil until soft and lightly browned. Add the rest of the ingredients and mix well, then let it bubble and thicken in the pan. Taste and adjust the flavour by adding more lime juice, chilli or soy sauce, according to personal preference. Add a little water to get a nice "pourable-but-only-just" consistency. This sauce will keep for a week in a sealed jar in the fridge. If reheating it add a little more water if necessary.

Thread 5-6 pieces of marinated meat on each skewer. Cook on a barbecue or on a lightly oiled heavy griddle pan or hotplate, turning regularly, until nicely browned (about 10 minutes). Serve with the peanut sauce.

Makes 10-12 skewers

1	rabbit (retain liver – optional)
1 tbs	seasoned flour
75g (3oz)	butter
150ml (¼ pint)	white wine
1	clove garlic, peeled and left whole (optional)
2 tbs	fresh tarragon leaves or
2 tsp	dried tarragon
½ tsp	Bovril – optional

Cut the rabbit into pieces and dust with seasoned flour. Melt the butter in a casserole and brown the rabbit quickly on all sides. Reduce the heat and add the white wine and the garlic, if using. Cover the casserole and simmer gently for about 45 minutes or until tender. When the rabbit is cooked, add the tarragon leaves (if using dried, soak them first for 30 minutes in water and drain). Stir well so that all the leaves are moist and cook for about another 5 minutes. Take out the garlic. The liver may be sautéed in butter, chopped and added to the sauce before serving. For a fuller flavour add ½ tsp Bovril.

Serves 4

RABBIT WITH BLACK GRAPES AND TOMATOES

1	rabbit
3 tbs	oil
2	onions, chopped
3	sticks celery, chopped
2 tbs	flour
150ml (¼ pint)	red wine
275ml (½ pint)	stock
1	small tin tomatoes
1 tsp	tomato purée
	salt and pepper
1	clove garlic, crushed
	a splash of Worcestershire sauce
1 tsp	mixed herbs
225g (8oz)	seedless black grapes
225g (8oz)	tomatoes

Cut up the rabbit into pieces, brown well in oil, remove and keep warm. Soften the onions and celery in the pan, add the flour and brown lightly. Add the wine, stock, tinned tomatoes, tomato purée, seasoning, garlic, Worcestershire sauce and herbs. Bring to the boil, add the rabbit and cook in a slow oven (150°C, 300°F, Gas Mark 2) for about 1¼ hours. Add freshly cut tomatoes and black grapes to serve.

Serves 4

If preparing the rabbit at home, retain 4 tbs of blood for the gravy. Mix 1 tbs of the gravy into the blood, then incorporate this gradually into the remaining gravy.

HARE

There are two species of hare in Britain, the brown and the mountain hare, which in Scotland is called the blue hare. Hares are a minor shooting quarry and most hare shoots are designed to prevent crop damage. While there is no close season, it is illegal to sell hare between March 1 and July 31, though they are available frozen from gamedealers and farm shops all year round.

A young hare can be identified by its soft thin ears, which tear easily, its small, sharp, white teeth and its smooth coat. Older hare have large yellow teeth, a wavy coat and more pronounced lip.

Young hares are best roasted, while older ones are better marinaded then casseroled or jugged. An average brown hare will feed up to 6-8 people.

Hares should be hung head down, ungutted, for one to two weeks; as always, the time depends on the weather and personal taste. If the blood is needed for the recipe, place a bowl underneath the hare to catch it. A teaspoon of vinegar in the bowl stops the blood from congealing. Hare lose about one-third of their weight when they are cleaned.

If a hare is rather over-hung or musty inside, wash it in Milton sterilising fluid or vinegar.

For preparation details see page 270.

Wine recommendation

Hare requires full-bodied red wines with good direct fruit such as Gigondas from southern Rhône, or Barbaresco from Piedmont in north-west Italy. For hare marinated in wine and brandy, a Châteauneuf-du-Pape, also from the southern Rhône, would be best suited to complement the stronger flavours.

MARINADE
FOR HARE

(sufficient for a whole hare)

1	bottle red wine
6 tbs	olive oil
1	small sliced onion
5	juniper berries, crushed
1	clove garlic, crushed
1	bay leaf
	a little thyme
	black pepper

Combine the ingredients and use according to individual recipe.

The older the hare the stronger or more acid the marinade should be. Wine vinegar, lemon juice or brandy, in smaller quantities, can be substituted for the red wine. Only half the quantity of marinade will be needed for a saddle.

ROAST
SADDLE OF HARE

	marinade (see left)
1	saddle of hare
	lard, bacon fat, dripping or butter
	french mustard (optional)

For the gravy:

	strained marinade or red wine
	extra mustard or single cream

Marinate the saddle for 24 hours. Either lard the saddle or cover well with bacon fat, dripping or butter, and French mustard if using. Place in a hot oven (200°C, 400°F, Gas Mark 6), baste frequently and cook for about 35 minutes. Remove the saddle and keep warm.

To make the gravy, heat the pan juices and add the strained marinade or plain red wine, and a little mustard or cream. Stir well and serve separately.

Serves 3-4

ROAST HARE

1	hare
	marinade (see left) – optional
	salt and pepper
	French mustard, to taste
2 tbs	melted butter
450ml (¾ pint)	beef stock
2-3	juniper berries

For the gravy:

2	egg yolks
1 tsp	cornflour
3 tbs	cream
	a dash of Worcestershire sauce
	salt and pepper
2 tbs	port – optional

Prepare the hare by cutting off the back legs, then cut the ribs lengthwise as close to the meat of the back as possible. Leave the back in one whole piece. The head, front legs and ribs can be used for stewing. The roast back of a hare will serve four, but if there are more guests the back legs should be used as well.

They are prepared in the same way but take about 10 minutes longer to cook than the back.

The fine skin covering the meat must be taken off as well as the whitish-blue skin, which has to be removed with a sharp knife. (For older hare, marinate for 24 hours). Salt and pepper the prepared meat, and brush well with French mustard. Add the crushed juniper berries. Baste with the melted butter and roast in a moderate oven (180°C, 350°F, Gas Mark 4), basting frequently with the remaining butter, for ¾-1 hour. When all the butter has been used up, continue to baste with beef stock, adding a little at a time in order to intensify the flavour.

In a small saucepan mix all the gravy ingredients together, except the port, and add to the juices from the hare and bring to the boil before adding the egg mixture. Strain the gravy and add the port just before serving.

The hare can be served with stewed apple, cranberry sauce, potatoes and red cabbage.

Serves 6-8

JUGGED HARE
Hugh Fearnley-Whittingstall

Allow three hours preparation time.

1	large brown hare, skinned plus its blood (liver optional)
100g (4oz)	streaky bacon
2 tbs	olive oil
1	small onion or 3 shallots, peeled and sliced
1	large carrot, peeled and sliced
1 rounded tbs	plain flour
25g (1oz)	butter
½ bottle	good (aged) elderberry wine or full-bodied red wine such as merlot or Cabernet Sauvignon
	a few sprigs of thyme
	a few sprigs of wild chervil or parsley
2	bay leaves
	salt and freshly grounded black pepper
2	squares of bitter chocolate – optional

Joint the hare with a heavy knife or meat cleaver, cutting off its legs and dividing the saddle into 5-6 pieces.

Start to prepare the dish at least three hours before you intend to eat it. Chop the bacon into 1cm (½in) pieces and sweat for a few minutes in half the oil in a large frying-pan.

Add the onion and carrot and cook for a further few minutes. Transfer the bacon and vegetables to a large heavy casserole. Put the frying-pan back on the heat and add the butter and the rest of the oil. Turn the pieces of hare in the flour, then add to the pan. Fry hare until nicely browned, turning occasionally, and transfer to the casserole.

Pour over the wine and just enough water to barely cover the meat. Add the herbs, tied in a bundle, season with salt and pepper and bring the pan to a gentle simmer. Cover and cook over a gentle heat or in a slow oven (150°C, 300°F, Gas Mark 2) for 2-3 hours. The hare is cooked when the meat is tender and starts to come away from the bone.

Remove the hare from the casserole to a warmed dish. Strain the stock through a sieve to remove the vegetables, then return to the casserole over a low heat. Have the blood ready in a small basin, and spoon a little of the cooking liquid into the blood to both warm and thin it – stir well. Add the chopped liver (optional) and the grated chocolate to the casserole, then ladle in the warmed blood, a little at a time, stirring as you go.

When the sauce is smooth and well blended, return to the heat and bring back to the boil. Return the pieces of hare to the pot and bring back to a gentle simmer.

Serve with herb dumplings (see pg 267). Place the dumplings on top of the meat, cover the pot and allow to steam gently for 20 minutes.

Serves 8

SALSA DI LEPRE
Elizabeth David's hare sauce for noodles

legs of hare

For the marinade:

1	bottle of red wine
	(less one glass, see below)
1	onion, sliced
2	cloves of garlic, crushed
2	bay leaves
12	peppercorns
	sprig of rosemary
	sprig of sage
1	carrot, diced
	a few celery leaves
	lard or oil
	a handful of fresh herbs
2	carrots, diced
2-3	sticks of celery, chopped
100g (4oz)	lardons
1	glass of red wine
	cooked noodles

Combine the marinade ingredients, pour over the meat and leave for two days. Brown the meat in lard or oil in a casserole, add the fresh herbs, carrots and celery sticks and the lardons, then pour over a glass of red wine. Stew the hare very slowly until the meat is falling off the bones. Remove the meat from the bones and liquidize or put in a blender together with the remaining ingredients from the casserole. Keep the sauce warm and pour over the cooked noodles.

Serves 4-6

This is a good way of using the legs of a hare.

MARINATED HARE IN BEER

HARE MINUTE STEAKS

1	hare cut into serving pieces
450ml (¾ pint)	beer
1	clove garlic, crushed
1	bay leaf
450g (1lb)	onions, finely sliced
2 tbs	flour
50g (2oz)	beef dripping
275ml (½ pint)	stock
1 tsp	wine vinegar

Put the pieces of hare in a bowl with the beer, garlic, bay leaf and onions, and leave in a cool place to marinate for about 24 hours. Dry the pieces of hare, dredge them with flour and brown in the hot dripping – not too quickly. Place the pieces in a casserole, add the marinade, stock and vinegar, then bring to the boil. Cover, and cook in a moderate oven (180°C, 350°F, Gas Mark 4) for about 2 hours or until tender. If preferred cover the top of the casserole with thickly sliced boiled potatoes brushed with butter or dripping for the last 45 minutes.

Serves 6-8

Only suitable for young hare.

	butter for frying
2	steaks cut from the saddle, approximately 1x10x10cm (½x4x4in)
To serve:	brown mustard sauce (see page 242)

Beat the steaks with a rolling pin and then fry them in butter like any other steak. Serve with brown mustard sauce.

Serves 2

FILLETS OF HARE

Use the fillets from the saddle of a young hare. The rest of the animal can be used for soup, casserole or pâté.

2-3 tbs	oil
1	young hare
	salt and pepper
100ml (4fl oz)	wine

Either:

	a few sautéed mushrooms
2 tbs	tomato purée
1	small clove garlic, crushed

or

	a little sour cream
1 tbs	good quality redcurrant jelly

Cut the fillets in long thick slices down the back. If time allows, soak them in oil for an hour or so. Season with salt and pepper and fry gently in the oil, turning several times and adding more oil if necessary. As they must be well cooked they will take 20-30 minutes.

Halfway through the cooking time add the wine, mushrooms, tomato purée and garlic; alternatively at the end of the cooking time, remove the fillets and add a little sour cream and redcurrant jelly. Heat up the sauce but do not allow to boil. Pour over the fillets.

Serve with sauté potatoes or noodles.

Serves 2-3

VENISON

Like most game, venison is virtually fat-free and has a wonderful flavour that lends itself to a variety of cooking methods. It can be treated in much the same way as beef – with the haunch or saddle best for roasting, and steaks and chops fried or barbecued. The liver, too, when it is very fresh, makes excellent eating, quickly fried in butter.

Like beef, the flavour and texture of venison is improved if it is hung in a fly-proof, well-ventilated place for up to 2 weeks. Many consider the meat of the red deer to be superior – certainly it has the strongest flavour and needs hanging longer than other types – and it is red deer meat that will generally be found in a supermarket or butcher. However roe, fallow and sika are sometimes available, while the smaller deer – muntjac and Chinese water deer – though they make very good eating, are rarely sold.

The fat of a young animal is whiter than that of an older one, and the flesh is dark red and finely grained. If in doubt as to the age of a deer, it is advisable to marinate the meat.

The shooting seasons for deer vary according to species and sex (see page 279), but venison is widely available, fresh or frozen, from butchers, gamedealers and deer farms throughout the year.

Traditionally venison is eaten pink and, if it to be eaten hot, it should be served on very hot plates, otherwise the meat tends to look grey and unappetising.

Wine recommendation

As venison has such a powerful taste, a bigger and upfront wine is required such as a new world Cabernet Sauvignon from Australia or California or a mature and juicy red Bordeaux. For deer with anchovies, the wine must be full-bodied and fruity to stand up to the strong flavours. An oaky Californian Cabernet Sauvignon will be a good choice.

ROAST VENISON

Venison carries on cooking long after it comes out of the oven. If it is a good enough leg or haunch to be roasted then it should not be overcooked. The first few slices may look very rare, but they will look less bloody when they have been on the plate for a few moments.

1	saddle or haunch of venison
	pork fat or bacon for larding
	olive oil
	marinade (optional – see page 262)
2 tbs	flour
275ml (½ pint)	marinade or red wine
2 tsp	tomato purée
	salt and pepper
150ml (¼ pint)	fresh or sour cream

Only marinate the meat if there is doubt about its age. The joint should be well larded with pork fat or bacon using a larding needle or by making little slits in the skin and pushing in the fat.

Rub the joint all over generously with the oil, loosely wrap it in foil and place in a moderately hot oven (190°C, 375°F, Gas Mark 5). Baste frequently, preferably every 10 minutes, and cook for 15 minutes per 450g (1lb) for a large joint, and 20 minutes per 450g (1lb) if it is smaller (under 1.8kg/4lb). This should make it slightly pink.

If the venison is to be eaten cold, cook it for a slightly shorter time as it will continue cooking as it cools and dries out.

To make the gravy: remove most of the fat from the pan and stir the flour into the pan juices. Add 275ml (½ pint) marinade (if using) or red wine, the tomato purée, salt and pepper, and cream. Stir well and heat until just bubbling.

Alternatively, pour off the fat and stir in some sour cream, a little redcurrant jelly and a squeeze of lemon.

Serves 6-8

If drinking good wine with venison, limit the amount of redcurrant jelly used. It may be good with the venison but it doesn't help the wine at all.

DANISH SADDLE OF YOUNG VENISON
WITH WALDORF SALAD

	saddle of young venison
	oil
	salt and pepper
275ml (½ pint)	**stock or beef cube and water**
	beurre manié
	Waldorf salad (see page 269)

Oil the joint well, sprinkle with salt and pepper and place in a roasting tin. Add stock so that it does not become dry when cooking. Place in a moderate oven (180°C, 350°F, Gas Mark 4), basting occasionally. Cook for 1¼-1½ hours, according to taste. Remove the meat from the oven and keep warm. Thicken the juices with a little beurre manié and serve with a Waldorf salad.

Serves 6-8

VENISON STEW
WITH POTATO DUMPLINGS

1.3kg (3lb)	diced shoulder of venison
50g (2oz)	butter
100g (4oz)	flour
1½ tsp	salt
570ml (1 pint)	stock
1.2 litres (2 pints)	hot water
1	onion
8	peppercorns
4	cloves
2	bay leaves
	juice of ½ lemon
150ml (¼ pint)	red wine

For the potato dumplings:

900g (2lb)	potatoes
10	slices bread
1 tsp	salt
¼ tsp	pepper
1	onion, grated
1 tsp	finely chopped parsley
2	eggs, well beaten
50g (2oz)	flour
1.75 litres (3 pints)	boiling salted water

Heat the butter, stir in the flour and cook until browned. Add the salt, stock and water, stir well, then add the onion, peppercorns, cloves, bay leaves and lemon juice, bring to boil and let boil for 5 minutes. Add the meat, bring back to the boil, turn down, cover and cook gently for 1¼ hours. Add the wine, stir and cook for another 15 minutes.

For the potato dumplings: wash, peel and grate the potatoes. Soak the bread in a little cold water and squeeze out as much water as possible. Mix the bread, salt, pepper, onions and parsley together, add the potatoes and eggs, mix well. Form into balls, roll in flour and drop into the boiling water, cover the pot tightly and boil for 15 minutes.

Serves 6-8

BELGIAN VENISON IN BEER WITH ONIONS

1.3kg (3lb)	cubed venison
3 tbs	oil
675g (1½lb)	onions, sliced
	salt and pepper
4	cloves garlic, crushed
275ml (½ pint)	beef stock or tinned consommé
570ml (1 pint)	light beer
2 tbs	brown sugar
1	bouquet garni
1½ tbs	arrowroot or cornflour
2 tbs	wine vinegar

Brown the venison in hot oil in a frying-pan, a few pieces at a time. Remove the meat, reduce the heat and stir in the onions, adding more oil if necessary. Brown lightly, stirring frequently, for about 10 minutes. Add salt, pepper and garlic. Arrange the venison and onions in layers in a casserole.

Heat the stock in a frying-pan, then pour over the venison and onions. Add the beer to cover. Stir in the sugar and put in the bouquet garni. Bring to a simmer, cover, and place in a moderately slow oven (170°C, 325°F, Gas Mark 3) for 2 hours, or longer, depending on the quality of the venison.

When cooked, drain off the liquid, skim off the fat, beat in the arrowroot or cornflour mixed with vinegar, and simmer for a few minutes. Pour the sauce over the meat.

Serves 6

BARBECUED VENISON STEAK

| 4 | venison steaks |
| | a little flour |

For the marinade:

150ml (¼ pint)	red wine
2 tbs	French mustard
1 tbs	soft brown sugar
2 tbs	tomato purée
1 tbs	chilli powder
2	small onions, sliced
2	cloves garlic, crushed, lightly fried in oil

Thoroughly mix all the ingredients for the marinade in a blender. Pour over the meat and leave, covered, for 24 hours, turning occasionally. Drain the meat from the marinade and dust with flour.

Barbecue over the faintly glowing embers of a dying charcoal fire, basting from time to time with the marinade.

Serve with baked potatoes and salad.

Serves 4

MINUTE VENISON STEAKS
in Francatelli's sauce

Francatelli was Queen Victoria's chef.

4	venison steaks, cut thinly
	butter for cooking
2 tbs	port
225g (8oz)	good quality redcurrant jelly
	a few fresh redcurrants
	(or fresh cranberries, according to season)

Make the sauce by simmering the port and redcurrant jelly together for about 5 minutes. Sieve and keep warm.

Put a good knob of butter in a heavy frying-pan and heat until foaming. Flash the steaks in the butter, cooking very quickly on each side, and season according to taste. Serve immediately with the sauce and a few redcurrants or cranberries scattered over.

Serves 4

VENISON KEBABS WITH YOGHURT & CUCUMBER SAUCE

450g (1lb)	good quality venison, cubed
	olive oil for basting

For the marinade:

2.5cm (1in)	piece of fresh ginger
2	cloves of garlic
½ tsp	ground turmeric
½ tsp	ground cumin
¼ tsp	chilli powder
¼ tsp	ground cinnamon
6	black peppercorns, crushed
2	cloves
1 tbs	olive oil
2 tbs	plain yoghurt

For the sauce:

½	cucumber
275ml (½ pint)	plain yoghurt
¼ tsp	ground cumin
	a few drops of lemon juice
	a few chopped mint leaves
	salt and pepper to taste

Chop the ginger and garlic and combine until they form a paste. Add the remaining marinade ingredients, stir well and pour over the cubed venison. Leave the meat to marinate for a few hours in a cool place.

Drain the meat and thread onto skewers so the cubes do not touch. Grill or barbecue for about 15 minutes, turning from time to time and basting with olive oil.

For the sauce: Coarsely grate the cucumber onto a plate, sprinkle with salt and leave for half an hour. Press the cucumber and pour away the excess liquid. Stir into the yoghurt and add the ground cumin, chopped mint leaves and lemon juice. Season to taste.

Serves 4

MARINATED BRAISED VENISON

2.7kg (6lb)	saddle of venison

For the marinade:

½-¾ bottle	red wine
6-8 tbs	olive oil
1	onion, sliced
2	carrots, sliced
1	clove of garlic, crushed
	pepper
6	juniper berries, crushed
1	bay leaf
¼ tsp	thyme

225g (8oz)	lardons
4 tbs	butter
4 tbs	olive oil
	beurre manié
70ml (2½fl oz)	port
1-2 tbs	redcurrant jelly
	salt and pepper

Combine the ingredients for the marinade and leave the venison to marinate for 3-4 days, turning several times a day. Brown the lardons in butter and oil until crisp, remove, then brown the venison. In a small saucepan, reduce the marinade to about half and pour over the meat, add the lardons, cover tightly and cook in a moderately slow oven (170°C, 325°F, Gas Mark 3) until tender, about 1½ hours.

Remove the meat and keep warm.

Reduce the sauce slightly, thicken with beurre manié, add the port and redcurrant jelly, season to taste, mix very well and strain over the venison.

Serves 6-8

CIVET OF VENISON

Jane Grigson

1.3kg (3lb)	stewing venison, diced and trimmed

For the marinade:

½ bottle	red wine
1	medium onion, sliced
3 tbs	brandy
3 tbs	olive oil
	salt and black pepper

For the sauce:

25g (1oz)	butter
225g (8oz)	lardons
2	large onions, chopped
1	large carrot, diced
1	large clove garlic, crushed
2 tbs	flour
	beef or venison stock
	bouquet garni
100g (4oz)	mushrooms, sliced

For the garnish:

100g (4oz)	butter
2 tsp	sugar
24	button onions
	beef or venison stock
24	small mushrooms
	salt and pepper
8	slices bread
	chopped parsley

Mix the marinade ingredients together, season well and soak the venison in it overnight.

Melt the butter in a heavy pan and brown the lardons in it. When the fat runs from the lardons, put the onions, carrot and garlic into the pan to be browned slightly, then the well-drained venison. Stir the flour into the pan to take up the fat, and make a sauce by adding the strained marinade, plus enough stock to cover the ingredients. Add the bouquet garni. Transfer to a deep casserole if this is more convenient.

VENISON LIVER
FRIED IN BUTTER AND SAGE

Add the mushrooms and simmer until the venison is cooked, about 1½-2 hours or cook in the oven (170°C, 325°F, Gas Mark 3) for 1½-2 hours. Skim off any surplus fat. (The cooking up to this point may be done the day before).

Half an hour before the meal, prepare the garnish and reheat the civet if necessary. Melt 25g (1oz) of butter with the sugar in a heavy pan. Turn the small onions in this until they are well coated. Add just enough stock to cover them and cook at a galloping boil. This will reduce the liquid to a spoonful or two of caramel. Be careful it doesn't burn, and keep shaking the onions so that they are nicely glazed. Cook the mushrooms in 25g (1oz) of the butter, with salt and pepper.

Cut the bread into triangles, and fry in the remaining butter.

Arrange the civet on a large hot serving dish, put the mushrooms and onions on top, pushing them down a little so that they look naturally part of the dish. Put the croutons round the edge, sprinkle with parsley and serve very hot.

Serves 8

This follows a traditional Italian recipe for calves' liver and works especially well with the mild taste of roe liver.

6	**large but thin slices of venison liver**
3-4	**shallots, chopped**
	butter for frying
12-16	**whole sage leaves**

Gently fry the shallots in butter for about two minutes then push to the side of the pan. Turn up the heat and quickly fry the liver on both sides, leaving it just pink in the middle. Remove the liver to warmed plates and fry the sage leaves until they start to colour (about a minute).

Then pour the shallot and sage mixture over the liver, and serve with new potatoes and spring cabbage.

Serves 2

It is hard to do this well for more than two people as the ingredients tend to stew rather than fry if the pan is too full.

MARINATED DEER
À LA CAJSA WARG

Cajsa Warg was the first woman in Sweden to publish a cook book, in 1755. This recipe is slightly modernised.

For the marinade:

570ml (1 pint)	vinegar
570ml (1 pint)	water
1	bay leaf
2	celery stems
2	cloves
2	cloves garlic, crushed
2	onions, sliced
2	carrots, sliced
4	juniper berries, crushed

1.3kg (3lb)	roasting venison
2 tbs	flour
2 tsp	salt
75g (3oz)	butter
1 tbs	anchovy sauce
150ml (¼ pint)	beef stock or water
¼	lemon
100g (4oz)	mushrooms
2	cloves

Bring all the ingredients for the marinade to the boil, then cool quickly. Put the meat in a deep bowl and pour over the marinade. Allow to stand for at least 24 hours, turning the meat a few times. Take out the meat and pat it dry. Mix the flour and salt together and coat the meat in the mixture until evenly covered. Melt the butter in a pan and fry the meat until brown all over. Add the anchovy sauce, beef stock or water, and some of the marinade. When the meat is half ready, take it out and cut it into serving pieces. Put it back in the pan, add the mushrooms, and ¼ lemon stuffed with cloves. Cover and let simmer until the meat is tender. Add more beef broth or water if necessary.

Take out the lemon with cloves. Put the meat on a serving dish and serve the gravy separately.

Serves 4-6

VENISON STEAKS

IN SOUR CREAM & RED WINE

GRILLED FILLETS OF VENISON

4	thick venison steaks
3 tbs	butter
	salt and pepper
	crushed juniper berries
½	onion, grated
150ml (¼ pint)	beef stock or tinned consommé
150ml (¼ pint)	red wine
150ml (¼ pint)	sour cream
	good quality redcurrant jelly

Melt the butter in a thick frying-pan, sprinkle steaks with salt and pepper and crushed juniper berries, and brown in butter; cook for about 4 minutes each side, according to taste. Remove and keep warm.

Turn down the heat and add the grated onion, mix well with all the bits left in the pan, add the stock and wine, and cook gently until the sauce has thickened. Add the sour cream and a little redcurrant jelly, simmer and strain over the steaks.

Serves 4

A few sautéed mushrooms can be scattered on top.

4	fillets of venison 1-2cm (1/2-3/4in) thick
	olive oil
	Freshly ground black pepper
	A little rosemary or thyme (optional)

Pour olive oil over the steaks and sprinkle with pepper and herbs, if using; leave for an hour or two. Grill for 3-5 minutes on each side and serve with redcurrant jelly or sauce poivrade (see page 243)

Serves 4

BREADED VENISON CUTLETS

8	venison cutlets taken from leg or loin
5 tbs	olive oil or cooking oil
	seasoned flour
1	egg, well beaten
	fine dry breadcrumbs
75g (3oz)	butter
8	large mushroom tops
	finely chopped parsley (optional)
100g (4oz)	good quality redcurrant jelly

Soak the cutlets in oil for about an hour. Drain them well, dredge with seasoned flour, dip in beaten egg and then cover with breadcrumbs, patting them on well. Sauté in 40g (1½oz) of the butter for 10-12 minutes, adding more butter or a little oil if necessary. Turn the cutlets frequently and, when cooked, transfer them to a warm platter. Sauté the mushroom tops in the remaining butter and place on each cutlet. Sprinkle with finely chopped parsley.

Mix the redcurrant jelly with the pan juices, bring to the boil and serve with the cutlets.

Serves 4

BONED LOIN OF VENISON IN SAUCE POIVRADE

675g (1½lb)	boned loin venison or slices from the haunch
2 tbs	olive oil
75ml (3fl oz)	red wine
	pepper
900ml (1½ pints)	sauce poivrade (see page 243)
50g (2oz)	raisins – optional
2 tbs	peanuts or cashew nuts – optional
	hot oil for frying
	croutons

Cut the meat into 2cm (¾ in) thick strips. Place them on a platter, pour the wine and the olive oil over them, sprinkle well with pepper and leave for an hour or two. Meanwhile make the sauce poivrade, adding a few soaked raisins and/or peanuts or cashew nuts to the sauce if using. Dry the meat well and fry in the hot oil for a few minutes (the meat will continue to cook on its way to the serving table). Place the meat on a hot platter, spoon a little of the sauce over and serve the rest separately. Croutons of fried bread may be placed around the serving dish.

Serves 4

VENISON CUTLETS IN THE ARDENNES STYLE

Elizabeth David

8	cutlets or 4 thick loin chops
12	crushed juniper berries
	a little dried marjoram or thyme
	salt
	freshly ground black pepper
	juice of ½ lemon
50g (2oz)	butter
1	small onion, chopped
2	carrots, diced
	small glass white wine or vermouth
	small glass water
3 tbs	chopped cooked ham
75g (3oz)	breadcrumbs
	half a bunch of parsley, chopped
	extra butter
2 tsp	redcurrant jelly
	juice of half a bitter orange
	or a little dark marmalade

Mix the juniper berries with some dried marjoram or thyme, salt and pepper. Pour lemon juice over the meat and rub with the juniper mixture. Leave for an hour or two. Melt the butter in a shallow pan and add the onion and carrot. When they are golden brown, put in the meat and brown it on both sides. Pour in the wine or vermouth, and boil steadily to reduce it a little. Add the water. Put some chopped ham on top of each cutlet or chop (transfer them, if more convenient, to a shallow ovenproof serving dish), then some breadcrumbs mixed with the chopped parsley. Dab a little butter on top of the breadcrumbs and bake in a slow oven (150°C, 300°F, Gas Mark 2) uncovered. The time required will depend on the condition of the venison, varying from 1 to 2 hours. After about ¾ hour, pierce one of the chops gently with a skewer to see if it's nearly ready. When the meat is tender, pour off the juices into a wide pan (keep the meat warm in the oven, at a reduced temperature) and boil the juices down until the flavour is well concentrated. Stir in the redcurrant jelly and bitter orange juice or dark marmalade. Pour over the cutlets. Serve very hot, with a few boiled potatoes. Serves 4

VENISON BURGERS

VENISON STEAK STROGANOFF

As venison lacks the fat of beef which usually goes into a hamburger, add minced streaky bacon or pork sausagemeat.

450g (1lb)	lean venison minced together with
225g (8oz)	streaky bacon or pork sausagemeat
2 tbs	breadcrumbs
1	egg, well beaten
	a little olive oil
	salt and pepper
1	onion, chopped
1	slice streaky bacon per burger – optional
	hot fat for frying

Mix all the ingredients together, apart from the bacon rasher, if using, and the fat and form into flat round cakes. Wrap each burger in streaky bacon, if using, secured with a toothpick. Fry in hot fat until well browned on both sides. Remove from the pan. Serve with gravy made by adding a little stock, redcurrant jelly and a squeeze of lemon to the pan or serve in a bap with ketchup or mustard.   Serves 4

450g (1lb)	venison fillet
2 tbs	butter
225g (8oz)	mushrooms, thickly sliced
1	small onion, chopped
1 tsp	Dijon mustard
150ml (¼ pint)	sour cream
2 tbs	brandy
	salt and pepper
	freshly chopped parsley

Cut the meat into strips 2.5cm by 5mm (1in by ¼ in). If possible, cut it across the grain. Melt the butter in a heavy pan and cook the onion gently for about 5 minutes; do not brown. Add the mushrooms and cook for a further 2 minutes. Add the meat, season well and stir in the mustard. Fry briskly for 2-3 minutes, according to taste. Stir in the brandy and sour cream and heat through gently. Adjust seasoning and sprinkle with parsley. Serve with noodles or rice.

Serves 4

VENISON AND TOMATO COBBLER

Angela Humphreys

675g (1½lb)	stewing venison, cubed
25g (1oz)	flour
	salt and pepper
1 tsp	cinnamon
2 tbs	oil
1	large onion, finely chopped
275ml (½ pint)	beef stock
225g (8oz)	tomatoes, skinned and sliced
1 tsp	basil
	black pepper

For the scone mixture:

225g (8oz)	self-raising flour
½ tsp	salt
50g (2oz)	margarine
150ml (¼ pt)	cold milk
1	egg, beaten

Toss the venison in the flour, seasoned with salt, pepper and cinnamon. Place in a casserole and brown in heated oil, then add the chopped onion, tomatoes, basil and pepper and stir in the stock. Bring to the boil, cover and cook in a moderate oven (180°C, 350°F, Gas Mark 4) for 2 hours or until the venison is tender.

To make the scones: sift the flour and the salt into a mixing bowl. Rub in the margarine. Make a well in the middle of the flour and pour in the cold milk. Mix quickly to a soft dough with a palette knife. Roll the dough out into rounds.

Remove the casserole and increase the oven temperature to (220°C, 425°F, Gas Mark 7). Place the scones on top of the meat and brush with the beaten egg. Bake near the top of the oven for 20 minutes, until well risen and brown.

Serves 4-5

VENISON LIVER AU POIVRE

225-350g (8-12oz)	venison liver
	flour
3-4 tbs	peppercorns, crushed
	olive oil

Slice the liver as thinly as possible, toss in flour and coat in the crushed peppercorns. Heat the oil in a frying-pan and flash fry the liver for a minute or two.

Serve with sauté or new potatoes and a green salad.

Serves 2-3

STALKER'S BREAKFAST

Especially good with roe liver – the fresher the better.

2-3	thin slices of venison liver
2	kidneys, halved
	salt and pepper
	butter
2-3	rashers of smoked bacon
1	tomato
To serve:	hot buttered brown toast

Season the liver and kidneys with salt and pepper to taste. Heat the butter in a frying-pan until foaming and fry the liver and kidneys quickly, until just pink in the middle.

Meanwhile, grill the smoked bacon and tomatoes. Transfer liver, kidneys, bacon and tomato to a warm plate and serve with hot buttered brown toast.

Serves 1

SWEDISH BRAISED VENISON

2.7kg (6lb)	leg venison
	strips of fat pork or bacon
	oil
275ml (½ pint)	stock
275ml (½ pint)	cream, fresh or sour
1 tbs	arrowroot or cornflour
1 tbs	blackcurrant or redcurrant jelly
	salt and pepper

Remove the outer membranes from the meat and lard with strips of fat pork or bacon. Brown the meat quickly over a high heat in oil. Lower heat, add the stock and cream, place uncovered in a moderately slow oven (170°C, 325°F, Gas Mark 3) for 2½ hours, basting frequently.

When the meat is cooked and tender, remove to a platter, skim the fat from the juices and strain them. Mix a paste of arrowroot or cornflour and water, add this to the juices and heat, stirring, until smooth and thickened. Add jelly and season to taste.

Carve the meat and serve with blackcurrant or redcurrant jelly, tomatoes and cucumber in vinegar, and roast potatoes.

Serves 8

FISH

There is something of the hunter-gatherer in most of us and for anglers providing a meal, however modest, at the end of a day's fishing is the ultimate satisfaction. From the seasoned angler who finally lands a prized brown trout from a Scottish loch to a youngster's first mackerel during a seaside foray, the taste of that fish will be all the more delicious for having been caught and brought home with pride.

Fish, once landed, must be treated with care and eaten as quickly as possible. They must be kept cool; a wicker creel with an ice pack works well, or wet weed can act as a cooler if no ice pack is available. Never leave a fish in the sun. Another tip is to keep the fish straight. Once it starts to stiffen, straightening it will tear the flesh. If your fish has been caught in muddy water, it is advisable to soak it in a mixture of 1 litre of fresh water to 2 tbs of wine vinegar and 1 tsp salt, changing the water as necessary.

For those who don't fish, local fishmongers and supermarkets offer ever more dazzling arrays of fish, all of which should be in good condition. Freshness is vital in fish and there are tell-tale signs to indicate how long it has been out of the water. Whole fish stay fresher longer than steaks or fillets so, whenever possible, buy a whole fish and cut it at home.

HOW TO TELL IF A FISH IS FRESH

The key points to look for are:

- Bright eyes – not cloudy or sunken
- Shiny, healthy scales – rough or dull scales indicate a stale fish
- Clean, fresh smell – fresh fish do not smell 'fishy'
- Flesh that feels resilient – fish go flabby when they are stale

The fish included in this section are a selection of those caught in British rivers, estuaries and in the harbour mouth. They are listed in alphabetical order. Fish is best served simply and should never be overcooked. Allow about 6oz of flesh per person. All recipes are for cleaned fish. For preparation details, see page 270.

Wine recommendations are on page 223.

In England and Wales, always check Environment Agency by-laws before taking fish from rivers.

BASS

BASS WITH LEMON BUTTER SAUCE

Bass has a wonderfully delicate flavour. Such is the popularity of this fish that it is now farmed in the same way as trout and salmon; this alleviates the pressure on wild stocks and enables the consumer to buy smaller fish which would otherwise be put back for conservation reasons.
Bass are usually cooked whole and can be baked or roasted and served with one of the savoury butters listed at the end of this chapter.

1	bass
25g (1oz)	butter
	salt and pepper
	a little plain flour
	a few sprigs of dill
½	lemon
	oil
	for the lemon butter sauce, see page 249

Dredge the fish with a little flour. Brush inside and out with melted butter and season well. Slice the lemon and place inside the cavity together with the dill. Take a large sheet of foil, smear with a little olive oil and place the fish in the centre. Gather up the edges and pinch together to form a loose parcel. Cook in a hot oven (200°C, 400°F, Gas Mark 6) for about 25 minutes, depending on the size of the fish. Remove from the oven and place on a warmed platter with the sauce served separately.

Bass can also be roasted; pour 2 tbs oil into a roasting tin, heat on the hob and fry the fish for a couple of minutes on each side until golden. Transfer to a hot oven for 20-25 minutes, basting frequently.

WHOLE BAKED BASS
STUFFED WITH MUSHROOMS

1	bass, about 1.3kg (3lb)
3 tbs	olive oil

For the stuffing:

4	cloves garlic, chopped
3 tbs	parsley
225g (8oz)	mushrooms, chopped
50g (2oz)	breadcrumbs
1	egg, beaten
	juice and zest of 1 lemon
1	glass of dry white wine
	salt and pepper

Oil a large piece of foil and lay the fish on it. Combine the stuffing ingredients and fill the cavity with the mixture. Mix the lemon juice and wine and pour over the fish, sprinkle with salt and pepper and pinch the edges of the foil together to make a loose parcel. Bake in pre-heated oven (200°C, 400°F, Gas Mark 6) for approximately 30 minutes, depending on the size of the fish.

BASS WITH WHITE WINE

1	bass, about 1.3kg (3lb)
1	sprig of lemon thyme
	a handful of parsley
	butter
1	onion, sliced into rings
1	red pepper, chopped
275ml (½ pint)	white wine
2 tbs	lemon juice
	salt and pepper
75g (3oz)	butter, cut into small pieces

Season the bass inside and out and place the thyme and parsley in the cavity. Butter a baking dish and cover the bottom with onion rings and red pepper. Place the fish on top, pour over the white wine and lemon juice and enough water to just cover the fish. Cover in foil and bake for about 30 minutes in a hot oven (200°C, 400°F, Gas Mark 6). Remove the fish and keep warm. Strain off the liquid and whisk in the butter until the sauce thickens and becomes creamy. Place the fish on a serving dish surrounded by the onion rings and red pepper; serve the sauce separately.

BREAM

MARINATED FRESHWATER BREAM WITH TARTARE SAUCE

Both freshwater and sea bream make good eating, though the former benefits from marinating. They must be descaled before eating and can be baked or roasted whole or pan-fried as fillets. Strong flavours such as bacon and anchovies work well with bream.

4	bream, filleted

For the marinade:

150ml (¼ pint)	olive oil
2-3 tbs	lemon juice
	a sprig of fennel or dill
2	cloves garlic, crushed
	salt and pepper
	seasoned flour or fresh breadcrumbs
	butter for frying

For the tartare sauce:

150ml (¼ pint)	good quality mayonnaise, or half salad cream and half crème fraîche
1 tsp	capers, chopped
1 tsp	chopped gherkins
1 tsp	freshly chopped parsley
1 tbs	lemon juice
1 tsp	vinegar – optional

Mix all the marinade ingredients together and cover the fillets of fish. Leave for 2-3 hours. Remove the fillets, dry on kitchen towel and dip in the seasoned flour or breadcrumbs until well covered. Melt the butter in a large frying-pan and, when foaming, fry the fillets for approximately five minutes, turning once. To make the tartare sauce: combine all the ingredients and mix well.

CARP

Carp has long since been eaten in eastern Europe, and is gaining in popularity in the UK too. It can be very muddy, so must be soaked in fresh water mixed with vinegar for several hours, or even a day or two, after cleaning.

It can be baked in foil with a little white wine or lemon juice and herbs, and is often accompanied by a sprinkling of fresh or ground ginger.

A strongly flavoured sauce is recommended.

Most recipes for carp work well for tench.

BAKED STUFFED CARP

1	carp
50g (2oz)	butter
1	onion, chopped
1	clove garlic, crushed
2	rashers of bacon, finely chopped
100g (4oz)	mushrooms, chopped
2tbs	chopped parsley
	salt and pepper
1 tbs	white wine or lemon juice
	a sprinkling of paprika

Melt the butter and soften the onion. Add the garlic and bacon, cook for 2-3 minutes then stir in the mushrooms, parsley, salt and pepper. Stuff the mixture into the fish's cavity, place on a large sheet of oiled foil and add 1 tbs white wine or lemon juice. Dot with butter or drizzle with a little olive oil and sprinkle with paprika. Bring the edges of the foil together to form a loose parcel and bake for about 30-40 minutes at 190°C, 375°F, Gas Mark 5.

CHAR

Arctic char, found in the deep lakes of northern England and Scotland, make excellent eating. Any recipe for trout will work equally well with char and it is particularly delicious when barbecued or potted.

FRIED CHAR

	char
25g (1oz)	butter (preferably clarified) for each fish
	salt and pepper
	lemon wedges to serve

Wash, clean and dry the char but do not remove the heads or tails. Heat the butter and, when foaming, cook the fish for 3-4 minutes on each side.

Season to taste and serve with lemon wedges.

CRAYFISH

This freshwater crustacean has the most delicious flavour. The native species (the white-clawed crayfish) is fully protected by law. The American signal crayfish is the commoner variety and may be caught and eaten, though it is illegal to move them to new waters. A crayfish sauce is the traditional accompaniment to quenelles de brochet (see under Pike.)

	a bucket of live crayfish
3 litres (5½ pints)	water
2 tbs	salt

For the aïoli:

3	cloves garlic, crushed
1 tbs	water
1	slice of white bread, crusts removed
1	egg yolk
150ml (¼ pint)	olive oil
1 tbs	lemon juice
	salt and pepper

Boil the water and add the salt. Plunge the crayfish into the water, bring back to the boil and cook for about 3-4 minutes. Strain, peel and remove the central vein (intestines) and serve. To make the aïoli: soak the bread in water, then squeeze dry. Combine the bread with the crushed garlic and beat in the egg yolk with a fork. Gradually add the oil, drop by drop, whisking all the time (a liquidizer or food-processor may be used) then stir in the lemon juice, salt and pepper to taste. A tablespoon of boiling water can be stirred in at the end.
Retain the crayfish shells to make a savoury butter.

SALAD OF PANCETTA & WARM CRAYFISH

4-6	rashers of pancetta
	a bucket of live crayfish
3 litres (5½ pints)	water
2 tbs	salt
	a selection of leaves, eg lambs lettuce,
	watercress, rocket
	dressing of 4 parts olive oil to
	1 part balsamic vinegar

Fry or grill the pancetta until crispy. Meanwhile, boil the water and add the salt. Plunge the crayfish into the water, bring back to the boil and cook for about 3-4 minutes. Strain, peel and remove the central vein.

Arrange a bed of leaves, toss over the crispy pancetta and crayfish, and drizzle with the dressing.

Fresh herbs and beer in the cooking liquor add to the flavour of the crayfish.

DACE

A small delicate fish which makes very good eating, especially cooked on a barbecue.

They can be cooked in the same way as trout or as part of a freshwater matelote (see pg 271).

DACE IN OATMEAL

An excellent breakfast dish

dace

seasoned oatmeal

butter for frying

Wash, clean and dry the fish and toss in the seasoned oatmeal.

Heat the butter and fry for a few minutes on each side.

EELS

Elvers (young eel) are very popular in Spain where they are cooked in olive oil and garlic; in Wales they are cooked in bacon fat and served with larva bread.

The fully-grown eel generally caught in the UK has traditionally been served cold in its own jelly or as eel pie. In fact eels can be cooked very simply, dipped in breadcrumbs and fried, and being fatty fish, are excellent for smoking too.

EELS WITH GREEN HERBS

4	small to medium eels cut into 5cm (2in) chunks
	butter for frying
1	shallot, peeled and finely chopped
1	celery stalk, finely diced
	a little white wine or dry cider
50g (2oz)	each of sorrel, watercress and nettle tops, roughly chopped
1 tbs	each of parsley and chervil, chopped
	salt and pepper

Fry the chunks of eel in the butter with the shallots and celery, then moisten with a little wine or cider. Toss in the herbs and cook for a few seconds until they have wilted. Season with salt and pepper

Serve with mashed potatoes.

SMOKED EEL
WITH WARM
POTATO SALAD

225-350 (8-12oz)	smoked eel
	oil for frying
1	onion, chopped
450g (1lb)	cooked new potatoes
4 tbs	groundnut or sunflower oil
1 tbs	white wine vinegar
1 tbs	Dijon mustard
	salt and pepper
	freshly chopped parsley
	a little warm water

For the potato salad, gently fry the onion in the olive oil. Add the potatoes and warm through. To make the dressing, place the mustard in a bowl with the salt and pepper and slowly whisk in a quarter of the oil a little at a time. Add the vinegar and slowly stir in the remaining oil. Thin down with a little warm water as necessary. Pour the dressing over the potatoes, while they are still warm, and serve with slices of smoked eel.

FLOUNDER

CRISPY FRIED
FLOUNDER

Flounders can be cooked in the same way as plaice.

8	flounder fillets
50g (2oz)	melted butter
1	egg
	salt
100-150g (4-5oz)	toasted breadcrumbs
	mixed with 2 tbs grated parmesan
To serve:	lemon wedges and tartare sauce
	(see page 185)

Beat the egg and add the melted butter and salt. Dip the fillets in the egg mixture and coat in the breadcrumbs and parmesan. Place on a baking sheet and cook in a hot oven (200°C, 400°F, Gas Mark 6) for about 15 minutes.

Serve with lemon wedges and tartare sauce.

GRAYLING

STUFFED GRAYLING

Grayling can be cooked in the same way as trout. They have large scales which need to be removed before cooking; this must be done with care in order not to bruise the flesh.

4	grayling
8 tbs	white wine

For the stuffing:

1 tbs	butter
50-75g (2-3oz)	mushrooms, chopped
	bunch of spring onions, chopped
225g (½lb)	fresh sorrel or 75g (3oz) frozen spinach
	salt and pepper

Melt the butter in a frying-pan and gently fry the mushrooms for 2-3 minutes. Add the spring onions and the sorrel and wilt for about a minute (if using frozen spinach, heat in butter in a separate pan, and sieve to remove excess water) and add salt and pepper. Divide the mixture into four and stuff the cavity of each fish carefully.

Take four large squares of foil and brush with oil. Place a fish on each square, draw up the edges of the foil and pour 1-2 tbs white wine over each. Pinch the edges together to form a loose parcel and place in a hot oven (200°C, 400°F, Gas Mark 6) for about 15-20 minutes.

GREY MULLET

GREY MULLET PROVENÇALE

A much underrated fish, grey mullet can be served baked, stuffed, grilled or steamed. They may need soaking to get rid of any mud and must be descaled before cooking. The roe can be smoked and mixed with cream cheese, olive oil and lemon juice to make a taramasalata.

1	grey mullet
1 tbs	olive oil
1	onion, chopped
1	clove garlic, crushed
400g (14oz)	tin of tomatoes or
6	fresh tomatoes, skinned and chopped
2 tbs	parsley, chopped
	a little fresh or dried basil or marjoram
	a little sugar
	salt and pepper
50-75g (2-3oz)	breadcrumbs
1 tbs	parmesan, grated
	butter

Heat the oil and sauté the onion until soft but not brown; add the garlic, tomatoes, herbs, sugar and seasoning. Place the fish in a buttered shallow dish and cover with the tomato mixture. Cook in a hot oven (200°C, 400°F, Gas Mark 6) for 30 minutes. Halfway through the cooking, remove from the oven and cover with the breadcrumbs and parmesan. Dot with butter and continue to cook for the remaining 15 minutes.

If preferred, this can be cooked in a foil parcel with the breadcrumbs omitted.

SADDLE OF GRIDDLED MACKEREL FILLETS
WITH SUN-DRIED TOMATOES & FENNEL SEEDS
Rick Stein

3 tbs	olive oil
2 tsp	lemon juice
1 tsp	chopped thyme
1 tsp	fennel seeds, lightly crushed
	a pinch of dried chilli flakes
4	275-350g (10-12oz) mackerel, filleted
25g (1oz)	rocket
25g (1oz)	prepared curly endive
15g (½oz)	flat-leaf parsley leaves
15g (½oz)	chervil sprigs
4-6	sun-dried tomatoes in oil,
	drained and thinly sliced
1 tbs	sherry vinegar
	salt and freshly ground black pepper

Mix together the olive oil, lemon juice, thyme, fennel seeds, chilli flakes, ½ teaspoon of salt and a few twists of freshly ground black pepper. Brush a little of this mixture over both sides of the fish fillets and set aside for 5 minutes. Toss the rocket, curly endive, parsley and chervil together and divide between 4 plates.

Heat a flat or ridged cast-iron griddle over a high heat until smoking-hot. Add the fillets, skin-side down and cook for 1-1½ minutes, turning them over halfway through. Transfer them to a plate to stop them cooking further. Break them into 7.5cm (3in) pieces. Arrange the pieces of fish and the strips of sun-dried tomato in among the salad leaves, taking care not to flatten the leaves too much. Add the remaining marinade and the sherry vinegar to the pan and swirl it around briefly. Spoon a little over the salad and the rest around the outside of the plate and serve straightaway.

Garfish or gurnard can be substituted for mackerel.

MACKEREL

GRILLED MACKEREL
WITH MUSTARD

*Fresh mackerel can be cooked in a wide variety of ways –
baked, roasted or grilled whole or fried as fillets. They are
excellent smoked and then eaten plain or as pâté and can
also be made into gravad lax, see page 212.*

1   mackerel

    oil or melted butter

    Dijon mustard

Score each side of the whole mackerel two or three times and
brush well with oil or melted butter. Put a little Dijon mustard
inside each slit. Cook under a hot grill for about 10-15 minutes,
turning once and basting from time to time.

*Alternatively wrap the mackerel in foil and cook in a
moderately hot oven (190°C, 375°F, Gas Mark 5) for 15
minutes.*

MACKEREL
WITH GOOSEBERRIES

*A perfect combination – the sharpness of the fruit contrasting
with the oily fish.*

8   fresh mackerel fillets

225g (8oz)   gooseberries

15g (½oz)   butter

    a little sugar, to taste

    black pepper

Wash, top and tail the gooseberries and cook in just enough
water so they don't stick to the pan, or microwave until just
tender. Add the butter. Purée in a food processor or liquidizer.
Add a little sugar if necessary, but it should taste tart.

Rinse and pat dry the fillets, season with pepper. Put the fillets
under a hot grill and cook for 2-3 minutes, turning once. Serve
immediately with the sauce.

Serves 4

SMOKED MACKEREL FISHCAKES
Prue Coats

225g (8oz)	smoked mackerel fillets
225g (8oz)	mashed potatoes
1	shallot, finely chopped
1 tbs	finely chopped gherkin
1	hard-boiled egg, finely chopped
	a little lemon juice
1 tbs	sour cream
1 tsp	dried dill
	salt and pepper
	flour to dredge
1	egg, beaten
	fresh brown breadcrumbs
	oil for frying

Skin the mackerel fillets and flake into a bowl; add the potato, shallot, gherkin, egg, lemon juice to taste, cream, dill, salt and pepper. Mix well, form into balls and flatten into cakes. Dredge with flour then coat with the egg and then the breadcrumbs. Heat some oil in a frying-pan and shallow fry until golden on each side.

Serve with a dill sauce (see page 249).

PERCH

FRIED FILLET OF PERCH

Perch can be cooked in the same way as trout. Often they are marinated in a mixture of olive oil and lemon juice first; sage goes particularly well with this fish.

As the skin of the perch is so thick, it is easier to fillet them, then lay the fillet flesh-side up and cut away from skin.

1	perch, filleted
	wholemeal flour
	a grating of nutmeg
	salt and pepper
	butter and oil for frying

Mix the wholemeal flour with the nutmeg, salt and pepper. Dip each fillet into the seasoned flour and shallow fry in the butter and oil for a few minutes on each side.

Serve with lemon wedges and anchovy butter (see page 222).

PIKE
QUENELLES DE BROCHET
(PIKE QUENELLES)

Pike is a round freshwater fish unfortunately not widely used in this country. Its 'Y'-shaped bones are difficult to remove but well worth the effort. Pike can be poached in a court bouillon and served with a horseradish sauce or filleted and baked in white wine or cider. Quenelles are perhaps the best-known way to prepare pike. Sauce nantua is the classic accompaniment to the quenelles although any herb-flavoured white wine sauce would work well too.

500g (1⅛lb)	pike fillet, skinned, filleted and de-boned
200g (7oz)	butter
2	eggs
4	egg yolks

For the panade:

125g (4½oz)	flour
4	egg yolks
90g (3½ oz)	butter
250ml (8fl oz)	milk
	salt, pepper and nutmeg

For the sauce nantua:

1 kg (2¼ lb)	unshelled raw crayfish, prawns or langoustines (or a mixture of the three)
	salt and pepper
2 tbs	olive oil
20g (¾ oz)	butter
1	carrot, peeled and finely diced
1	onion, peeled and finely chopped
½	fennel bulb, finely chopped
100ml (3½fl oz)	brandy
400ml (14fl oz)	dry white wine
	bouquet garni
	sprig of tarragon
1 tsp	tomato purée
3 tbs	crème fraîche
	beurre manié – 100g (4oz) butter to 25g (1oz) flour

Start this recipe the day before it is required.

To make the "panade", melt the butter in a saucepan and add the flour and egg yolks. Reduce the heat and pour in the milk, a little at a time, whisking vigorously until you get a soft paste very similar to choux pastry. Add salt, and plenty of pepper and a little grated nutmeg and cook for a further 5-6 minutes stirring all the time. Let the mixture cool and refrigerate overnight.

To prepare the sauce, wash the shellfish, add salt and pepper to taste and cook briskly in olive oil for about 2 minutes; reduce the heat, cover and simmer for a further 5 minutes. Shell, de-vein and put aside. Retain the shells and heads and process in a blender. Wipe the pan with kitchen roll, melt the butter and add the carrot, onion and fennel. Once soft, add the brandy and set alight. Add the white wine, bouquet garni, tarragon, tomato purée and processed shells. Cook over a moderate heat for a further 10 minutes and season to taste. Remove the majority of the pieces of shell with a slotted spoon and add the beurre-manié a little at a time to bind the sauce. Add the crème fraîche and sieve.

Stir in the cooked crayfish (for a smooth sauce, liquidize again). Check for seasoning and cool until needed.

To make the quenelles, cube the fillets, and place with the butter and the "panade" in a food-processor and blend for 3 minutes until it is a fine paste. Put the mixture in a large bowl and incorporate each egg and yolk one by one stirring with a wooden spoon. Pass through a sieve if needed and cool.

To shape the quenelles, either use quenelles moulds or take two dessertspoons to shape oval patties from the mixture, ensuring that the spoons are cleaned in a bowl of hot water after each one has been made. Alternatively, use a piping-bag with a large nozzle to make lozenge-shapes.

Poach the quenelles for 30 minutes by simmering in a large pan of salted water or fish stock. Remove from the liquid and drain carefully onto a tea towel. If using moulds, place in a bain-marie of simmering water in a moderate oven for about 30 minutes. Reheat the sauce and pour onto individual plates; place the quenelles on top and garnish to taste or place the quenelles in a gratin dish, cover with the sauce and reheat for a few minutes in the oven before serving.

SALMON

Salmon is considered by many to be the king among fish. While there are those who prefer to eat sea-trout or bass, the salmon, due mainly to its extraordinary lifecycle and the magical way it leaps, holds a great fascination. It is also the ultimate quarry for many anglers – though nowadays beats often adopt a catch-and-release policy to help conserve the wild stock (catch and release is mandatory in England and Wales until mid-June). The optimum time for catching a salmon is between February and August.

In recent years salmon farms have sprung up in great numbers and, as a result, salmon is available all year round at very reasonable prices. A commercially farmed salmon will have a less-developed tail and fins than its wild counterpart and the flesh may not be as firm or flavoursome, but at least they help alleviate the pressure on the wild stocks.

Salmon can be bought whole, as steaks (or darnes), fillets, escalopes or medallions. The tail-piece tastes wonderful and has no bones and can often be bought at a reduced price. If buying or cutting steaks, make sure they are not too thin. They need to be at least 2cm (¾ in) thick otherwise they dry out and become woolly.

POACHED SALMON

This is the traditional way to cook salmon which is to be served cold, dressed (decorated with cucumber or radish) and very often as the centrepiece of a buffet. If you do not have a fish kettle, a large saucepan or preserving pan will work just as well.

1	large salmon

Court bouillon for a large fish:

3 litres (5½ pints)	water
1 litre (1¾ pints)	white wine
275ml (½ pint)	wine vinegar
3	onions, stuck with 3 cloves in each
3	carrots
2	large celery stalks
2	bay leaves
5-6	large sprigs of parsley
1 tbs	salt

Bring all ingredients, except the salmon, to the boil and then simmer for about ½-¾ hour. Lower the salmon into the fish kettle on a trivet or place a plate on the bottom of the saucepan, make a sling of treble-thickness foil and lower the fish onto the plate, curving it to the shape of the pan. Increase the heat until it returns to a simmer, cover and cook, making sure it doesn't boil, for about 6-8 minutes per 450g (1lb).

If the flesh is wobbly, like jelly, the salmon is undercooked; it should just give a little as you press the fish – firm flesh means it is overcooked. Remove the fish and, if you wish to skin it, do so gently while it is still warm.

Serve the poached salmon in aspic if desired (see below), with one of the sauces for fish (see page 246) or cold dressed with cucumber or radishes.

To make aspic: reduce the court bouillon and strain. Clarify the liquid by beating an egg white and shell together with some of the liquid, and then returning this to the rest of the liquid. Cook slowly and stir for a few moments, then allow the egg to rise to the surface.

SALMON STEAKS
WITH SAVOURY BUTTER

Leave the pan over a very low heat for about 10 minutes, turning gently every few minutes, so that the egg goes across the top of the liquid, catching the particles. Line a sieve or colander with muslin or cheesecloth (a coffee filter works well) and very gently strain the liquid through this.

To steam rather than poach fish, use a fish kettle in which the fish just fits. Pour in a little wine and water to just cover the bottom of the pan – no more than 3mm (⅛in) – and bring to the boil. Place chives and sprigs of thyme in the cavity and season. Lower the fish in the trivet into the kettle and steam (a 2.7kg/6lb salmon will take about 30-35 minutes). When nearly cooked, push in a fork until it reaches the backbone; if juice comes out and sets like albumen, steam for another minute or two. Retain the liquor in the kettle to make a sauce.

salmon steaks

butter

savoury butter to serve (see pg 221)

Have the steaks cut fairly thick, about 2cm (¾in), and weighing about 175g (6oz). Wrap each steak in very well buttered or oiled foil. Be generous with the foil in order to have plenty around the edges to pinch together to prevent the juices from escaping. Bake in a moderate oven (180°C, 350°F, Gas Mark 4) for about 15-20 minutes. If the steaks are to be served cold, allow them to cool before opening the foil.

To grill salmon, brush with oil or melted butter and season. Leave to stand for 15 minutes then grill under a medium heat for about 3-4 minutes each side. Baste frequently.

SALMON BAKED IN FOIL

Nowadays many cooks prefer to bake a whole fish in the oven. By creating a parcel with the foil, the moisture and flavour is retained very efficiently.

1	salmon or sea-trout, approximately 1.3-1.8kg (3-4lb)
25-50g (1-2oz)	butter
150-275ml (¼-½ pint)	white wine
	fresh herbs such as bay leaves, thyme, lemon thyme or tarragon

Take a large sheet of foil and butter generously. Dry the fish and place in the centre of the foil with the herbs on top. Draw the edges of the foil up and pour in the white wine. Pinch the edges of the foil together to make a loose parcel. Cook in a moderate oven (180°C, 350°F, Gas Mark 4) for about 40-45 minutes.

Salmon can be barbecued successfully either in foil or in newspaper. For the latter, rub olive oil over the fish, place across the centre pages of a broadsheet newspaper and scatter with fresh herbs, salt and pepper. Add more olive oil, wrap up tightly and tie with string. Soak the paper in water and cook over a barbecue for about ¾-1 hour.

Alternatively large salmon can be cooked in the dishwasher. Fill the cavity with lemon juice and dill, parcel up in a double thickness of foil making sure that no water can get in. Lay the parcel flat in the dishwasher and cook on a full hot cycle (not pre-wash) and leave to cool down before opening the door.

For larger fish it is advisable to give them two cycles.

Open the foil carefully to check that it is cooked.

SALMON QUICHE

20cm (8in)	pastry case, baked blind
225-275g (8-10oz)	cooked salmon
	fresh or tinned asparagus
	(or spinach) – optional
4	eggs
150ml (¼ pint)	natural yoghurt
150ml (¼ pint)	cream
2 tbs	parmesan cheese, grated
1 tbs	lemon juice
	a grating of nutmeg
	salt and pepper

Put a layer of asparagus or spinach in the pastry case and add the flaked salmon. Beat the eggs and mix in the cream, yoghurt, parmesan cheese, lemon juice, nutmeg, salt and pepper. Pour into the pastry case, though not right to the top. Bake in a moderately hot oven (190°C, 375°F, Gas Mark 5) for 25-30 minutes, taking out halfway through and topping up the mixture if necessary.

SAUTÉED SALMON STEAKS WITH WHITE WINE

4	salmon steaks, each about 2cm (¾ in) thick
	seasoned flour
40g (1½oz)	butter
150ml (¼ pint)	dry white wine

Dust the steaks lightly with seasoned flour. Melt the butter in a heavy frying-pan and, when bubbling, cook the steaks quickly on each side. Pour in the wine, cook and simmer, basting frequently, for about 20 minutes.

Serves 4

SALMON FILLETS WITH PESTO

4   salmon fillets

4 tsp   red pesto (or coriander pesto)

4   slices Cheddar cheese

olive oil

freshly ground black pepper

Take 4 sheets of foil, at least 30cm (12in) square. Brush each fillet with olive oil and place in the centre of the foil. Season with pepper, spread 1 tsp of red pesto over each fillet, top with a thin slice of Cheddar cheese and pinch the edges of the foil together to form a loose parcel.

Bake in a hot oven (200°C, 400°F, Gas Mark 6) for about 15-20 minutes.

Serves 4

BAKED SALMON STEAKS IN CREAM

The thicker the steaks, the better they bake and it is preferable to use one large steak between two people; if serving one thinner steak per person, vary the cooking time accordingly.

2   salmon steaks, each 5cm (2in) thick, or 4 steaks 2.5cm (1in) thick

salt

275ml (½ pint)   sour cream

1 tbs   lemon juice

1 tbs   finely chopped dill leaves

1-2 tbs   Dijon mustard (optional)

finely chopped parsley

Sprinkle the steaks with salt and place in a baking dish. Mix the other ingredients together, except for the parsley, and pour over the steaks. Place in a moderate oven (180°C, 350°F, Gas Mark 4). A 5cm (2in) steak will take about 30 minutes. When cooked, sprinkle with parsley.   Serves 4

Sautéed sliced mushrooms or some shrimps may be added to this before cooking.

SALMON KEBABS

450g (1lb)	skinless salmon fillet, cut into 2.5cm (1in) cubes
4 tbs	olive oil
2 tbs	fresh lime juice
1 tbs	dry white wine
3 tbs	parsley, finely chopped
	salt and pepper
1	red pepper, deseeded and cut into 2.5cm (1in) squares
2	red onions, quartered
	lime quarters to garnish

Mix the olive oil, lime juice, wine, parsley and seasoning and pour over the salmon chunks. Leave to marinate in a cool place for about an hour.

Thread the salmon onto skewers, alternating with onion quarters and pieces of red pepper.

Cook on a barbecue, basting all the time, or cook under a medium grill for about 10 minutes. Serve with lime quarters.

Serves 4

SALMON PIE

900g (2lb)	salmon, cut into cubes with bones and skin removed
3 or 4	hard-boiled eggs – optional
225g (8oz)	shrimps – optional
1-2 tbs	grated onion
3 tbs	chopped parsley
	salt, pepper and paprika, to taste
570ml (1 pint)	velouté or béchamel sauce (see pgs 247/8)
100ml (4fl oz)	white wine, vermouth, sherry or Madeira
225g (8oz)	puff pastry
1	egg, beaten

Place the salmon, eggs and shrimps if using, onion, parsley, salt, pepper and paprika in a casserole and mix together. Make a velouté or béchamel sauce, add wine to it and pour over the mixture. Cover with puff pastry, brush with beaten egg and place in a hot oven (200°C, 400°F, Gas Mark 6) for about 30 minutes.   Serves 4

This can be topped with mashed potatoes instead of puff pastry.

SALMON KEDGEREE

SALMON FISHCAKES

This is a classic way of using up fish, and is particularly popular as a breakfast or brunch dish.

50g (2oz)	butter
½	onion finely chopped
450g (1lb)	salmon, flaked with bones and skin removed
4	hard-boiled eggs, sliced
350g (12oz)	cooked rice
2-3 tbs	chopped parsley
1-2 tsp	curry powder
	salt and pepper
3-4 tbs	cream

Fry the onion gently in the melted butter. Add the salmon and rice and heat gently. Add the eggs, salt, pepper, curry powder and chopped parsley, and mix well.

Finally stir in the cream and serve.

Serves 4

The proportions of fish and potato may be altered to taste.

225g (8oz)	salmon, with all bones and skin removed
350g (12oz)	mashed potatoes
	salt and pepper
1-2 tbs	single cream if the mixture is dry
2 tbs	finely chopped parsley
	flour
	fat for frying
	serve with hollandaise sauce (see pg 246)

Flake the salmon and mix with mashed potatoes. Season well and stir in the parsley. If the mixture is too dry, add a little cream until it will hold together without being sticky.

Shape into cakes of even size and dust them with flour.

Fry in hot fat until golden brown, making sure they are hot right through – about 5 minutes on each side.

Serve with hollandaise sauce.

KOULIBIAC
or RUSSIAN FISH PIE

450g (1lb)	cooked salmon
50g (2oz)	butter
1	onion, finely chopped
75g (3oz)	long-grain rice
200ml (8fl oz)	fish stock
100g (4oz)	mushrooms
2	hard-boiled eggs, quartered
2 tbs	lemon juice
2 tbs	chopped parsley
450g (1lb)	puff pastry
1	egg, beaten or a little milk
To serve:	sour cream and chives

Sauté the onion in half the butter and add the rice, stir until coated with butter and add the fish stock. Simmer for about 15 minutes until the rice is cooked.

Melt the rest of the butter in a pan and gently cook the mushrooms. Add the flaked fish, cooked rice, hard-boiled eggs and lemon juice. Add the parsley, season to taste and mix well. The mixture should be fairly dry – leave to cool.

Roll out the pastry and line a 20cm (8in) loose-bottomed cake tin. Spoon in the filling and top with the remaining pastry, sealing the edges well. Brush with beaten egg or milk and bake in a hot oven (220°C, 425°F, Gas Mark 7) for 30-35 minutes. Serve hot or cold with sour cream and chives.

Make into individual pies by rolling out small circles of pastry, putting a spoonful of the mixture over one half, brushing the edges with beaten egg or milk and folding over the pastry to make a pasty.

SEA-TROUT

DRESSED SEA-TROUT

Sea-trout or sewin are the sea-going version of the brown trout. They are much-prized by both the angler and the chef.

Sea-trout vary in size, but the smaller ones often have the better flavour, the flesh of larger fish tending to be somewhat pale.

Like so many fish, sea-trout is best cooked simply and most recipes for salmon and trout can be adapted for sea-trout. It is delicious smoked and many people consider smoked sea-trout to have a better flavour than smoked salmon.

1	sea-trout, approx 1.3-1.8kg (3-4lb)
25-50g (1-2oz)	butter
150-275ml (¼-½ pint)	white wine
	fresh herbs such as bay leaves, thyme, lemon thyme, dill or tarragon
	radishes and cucumber for decoration
	mayonnaise to serve

Take a large sheet of foil and butter generously. Dry the fish and place in the centre of the foil with the herbs on top. Draw the edges of the foil up and pour in the white wine. Pinch the edges of the foil together to make a loose parcel.Cook in a moderate oven (180°C, 350°F, Gas Mark 4) for about 40-45 minutes and, when cooked, remove the skin while still warm. Slice the radishes and cucumber very thinly with a mandolin and arrange over the fish to resemble fish scales. Serve with good quality mayonnaise.

GRAVAD LAX made from SEA-TROUT or SALMON

This Scandinavian dish is similar to smoked salmon but more moist and tender.

To every 900g (2lb) filleted fish add:

    3 tbs   salt

    3 tbs   sugar

    2 tbs   crushed white peppercorns

             plenty of dill

Clean and fillet the fish, but do not wash. Take a dish with sides which as nearly as possible fits the piece of fish. On the bottom spread a layer of the salt, sugar and pepper mixture, and a layer of dill stalks. Spread a layer of salt mixture on the cut side of each fillet. Put one fillet skin side down in the dish and cover with dill. Place the other fillet on top, cut sides together. Cover with the rest of the salt and some dill, then cover with foil. Make a few holes in the foil. Place a light weight on top and leave in a cool larder or refrigerator for 48 hours, turning the fish once and pouring off any excess liquid. It is then ready to eat. Scrape away the dill and pepper. Cut into slices as you would smoked salmon and serve with dill sauce (see pg 249) or sour cream and cucumber sauce (see pg 251), brown bread and butter.

Rainbow trout and mackerel can be prepared in this way too.

TROUT

Freshly caught trout – particularly wild brown trout – do not need elaborate treatment. They are superb simply grilled or sautéed with butter, parsley and lemon juice and to do more may seem like an insult.

However, fish bought from a supermarket or fishmonger may need a little help. Smoking is one alternative (see page 274) and fresh, warm, smoked trout is a real treat on its own or it can be used in pâtés and mousses to great effect. For preparation, see page 273.

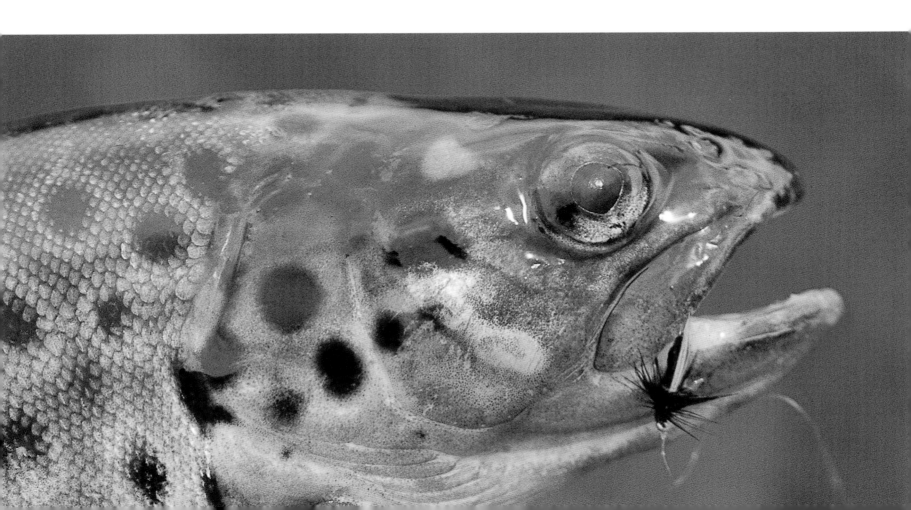

SAUTÉED
BROWN TROUT

TROUT
WITH BACON

This recipe is perfect for freshly caught brown trout, but be careful to heat the butter to the correct temperature. If it is too hot the skin of the fish will burn and ruin the taste, but if the butter is not hot enough the fish will lose its firmness.

A great breakfast dish.

1	small trout
3	strips thinly cut streaky bacon
	butter
	flour
	a little salt

trout

seasoned flour

butter, preferably clarified

parsley

lemon juice

Clean the trout and wipe it, then dust lightly in seasoned flour.

Heat the butter and fry for about 10-20 minutes depending on the size of the fish – turning every now and then.

Place on a serving dish, pour over any butter from the pan, and sprinkle with parsley. Either sprinkle with a little lemon juice, or melt some more butter in the pan, sprinkle lemon juice into it and then pour it over the fish.

If preferred, brown extra butter until it starts to smell nutty and pour over the fish.

Fry the bacon in butter until crispy; if necessary add a little more butter and, having dusted the trout in flour, fry in the fat for about 5 minutes each side. The bacon will probably provide enough salt, if not add a little more.

Alternatively toss the trout in seasoned oatmeal and fry in hot butter untill brown on both sides This should take about 8 minutes for a 275g (10oz) fish. If using fillets, cook for about 3 minutes on each side.

NUTTY TROUT
Angela Humphreys

2	rainbow trout, filleted
1 tbs	oil
1	small onion, finely chopped
75g (3oz)	wholemeal breadcrumbs
2 tbs	chopped parsley or thyme
50g (2oz)	chopped almonds
1 tbs	milk

Heat the oil and cook the onion gently until soft. Remove from the heat and stir in the breadcrumbs, herbs, milk and almonds. Place the fillets on a lightly oiled grill and cook under a medium heat for 5 minutes.

Divide the topping between the four fillets and cook for a further 4-5 minutes until the topping is crisp.

Serves 4

POACHED TROUT

A good way of cooking trout which is to be served cold.

4	trout

For the court bouillon:

1 litre (1¾ pints)	water
450ml (¾ pint)	white wine
70ml (2½fl oz)	wine vinegar
1	onion, stuck with 3 cloves
1	carrot, sliced
1	stalk celery
1	bay leaf
1	sprig thyme
2	sprigs parsley
	salt and pepper

Mix all the ingredients for the court bouillon, bring to the boil and simmer for about an hour before adding fish. Poach the trout gently in just enough court bouillon to cover. They won't need more than about 4-6 minutes. The more shallow the pot, the easier they will be to get out. Serve with any suitable sauce or with just browned butter.

Serves 4

TROUT MOUSSE

4	smoked or poached trout
6-8	stalks celery, finely chopped
25g (1oz)	gelatine
275ml (½ pint)	white wine or wine and fish stock
1	green pepper, blanched and diced
1 tbs	horseradish cream
	salt and pepper
275ml (½ pint)	lightly whipped cream

Discard all the skin and bones from trout. Flake the flesh carefully and mix with celery. Dissolve the gelatine in half of the white wine (or wine and fish stock) over a gentle heat, then add the rest of the liquid. Stir gently into the trout and celery (the fish should not become a mush). Add the green pepper and horseradish cream.

Season well. Fold in the cream and turn into a mould.

Serve with cucumber salad.

This may also be made with half-smoked trout and half-poached, or completely with smoked trout.

SMOKED TROUT & PANCETTA PASTA

Prue Coats

225g (8oz)	smoked trout
25g (1oz)	butter
1	shallot, peeled and finely chopped
100g (4oz)	pancetta, chopped
100g (4oz)	tomatoes, skinned, de-seeded and finely diced
	salt and pepper
450g (1lb)	tagliatelle
1 tbs	olive oil
275ml (½ pint)	single cream
1	egg yolk
	chopped parsley
	grated parmesan

Cook the shallot gently in the melted butter then add the pancetta. Stir for a few seconds and add the tomatoes. Season well and put to one side. Cook the pasta , strain and mix in the olive oil. Fork in the trout mixture. Beat the egg yolk into the cream and mix in at the last minute. Sprinkle with parsley and serve the parmesan separately.   Serves 4

TROUT EN CROUTE

4	rainbow trout, skinned and filleted
450g (1lb)	puff pastry
1	egg, beaten
	salt and pepper
	a little lemon juice

For the stuffing:

225g (8oz)	mashed potatoes
	rind and juice of 1 lemon
1 tbs	chopped chives
1 tbs	chopped tarragon
1 tbs	chopped parsley
1 tsp	powdered mace
	salt and pepper

Roll the pastry out thinly and cut into four rectangles (large enough to wrap around one fish). Blend all the stuffing ingredients together. Spread one quarter of the mixture on one side of each trout half and sandwich the other half on top. Place each of these in the centre of a pastry rectangle, season with salt and pepper and a squeeze of lemon juice. Dampen the edges of the pastry and fold over the fish, sealing with a little beaten egg. Brush the parcels with the remainder of the egg and lay on a lightly oiled baking sheet.

Bake for 20 minutes in a hot oven (200°C, 400°F, Gas Mark 6) then reduce the heat to (180°C, 350°F, Gas Mark 4) for a further 25 minutes. If the pastry starts to brown too quickly, cover with a sheet of greaseproof paper or foil.

Serves 4

BAKED TROUT WITH CREAM AND YOGHURT

6	small trout
	a little butter
150ml (¼ pint)	natural yoghurt
150ml (¼ pint)	double cream
50g (2oz)	ground almonds
1 tsp	ground turmeric
	salt and pepper

Clean the trout, wipe, but do not wash. Heat the butter and fry the trout quickly in an oven-proof casserole until just golden on the outside.

Mix together the yoghurt, double cream, ground almonds, turmeric and a little salt and pepper. Pour the mixture over the fish and bake in a moderately slow oven (170°C, 325°F, Gas Mark 3) for about 20 minutes or until cooked through.

Serves 6

HADDRELL'S TROUT

Angela Humphreys

1	trout
	a little butter
1 tbs	muscovado sugar
1 tbs	white wine
1 tbs	lemon juice
	salt and pepper

Sprinkle the fish with salt and pepper on both sides. Take a large sheet of foil, smear with butter and place the fish in the middle. Sprinkle the sugar inside the length of the cavity, draw up the edges of the foil and pour over the wine and lemon juice. Pinch together the edges of the foil to make a parcel and cook on a hot barbecue for about 10 minutes, depending on the size of the fish.

Serves 1

FRESHWATER FISH PLATTER

450g (1lb)	fillets of bream, tench,
	carp or perch, according to your catch
	butter for frying
1	crisp lettuce
225g (8oz)	cherry tomatoes
1	small tin of anchovies,
	drained and soaked in milk for ½ hour
4	hard-boiled eggs, quartered
225g (8oz)	fine green beans, trimmed and blanched
½	cucumber, diced
20	black olives
	a large handful basil

For the French dressing:

Mix together

4 tbs	olive oil
1 tbs	wine vinegar
1	clove garlic, crushed
1 tsp	French mustard
	a little sugar
	salt and pepper

Fillet the fish, making sure all the are bones are removed.
Heat the butter and pan-fry the fish gently, sprinkling with salt and pepper to taste, and remove.
Cover a large platter with lettuce, cucumber, cherry tomatoes and quartered eggs. Cut the cooked fish into strips and scatter, with the anchovies, over the salad. Garnish with black olives and torn basil leaves and drizzle with French dressing.

SMALL FRY FRY-UP
WITH RED PEPPER KETCHUP
Hugh Fearnley-Whittingstall

gudgeon, bleak, dace and other small fry

seasoned plain flour

2 eggs, beaten

breadcrumbs

oil for frying (sunflower or groundnut)

a little rock salt

chopped chives or

    a sprig of fennel – optional

For the red pepper ketchup:

2 red peppers

12 cherry tomatoes

1 tsp red wine vinegar

a little olive oil

salt and freshly ground black pepper

To make the sauce: roast, grill or barbecue the peppers until they are blackened. Put in a bowl, cover and leave to cool. Slice the tomatoes in half and grill until browned. Rub through a sieve. Peel the skin off the peppers, discard the seeds and finely dice the flesh. Mix the diced pepper with the tomato pulp, vinegar and olive oil, and season to taste.

Clean, gut and descale (not gudgeon) and remove the gills. Roll the fish in flour, dip in the beaten egg and coat with breadcrumbs.

Heat at least 5mm (¼ in) oil in a pan (or more in a deep-fat fryer) and fry the fish until golden brown.

Drain on kitchen paper, season with rock salt and garnish with chives or fennel. Serve with the red pepper ketchup.

FRESHWATER MATELOTE

900g (2lb)	perch, pike, tench dace or carp
25g (1oz)	butter
1	onion, thinly sliced
2	cloves garlic, crushed
225g (8oz)	mushrooms, sliced
3 tbs	Calvados or brandy
570ml (1 pint)	dry cider
1 tbs	chervil, chopped
	salt and pepper
	beurre manié

Fillet the fish and cut into 1in strips (goujons). Melt the butter and add the onion; cook until transparent then add the garlic and mushrooms and cook for a further 2-3 minutes. Pour in the Calvados or brandy (this can be set alight in a ladle first), the cider, chervil and salt and pepper. Bring to the boil, then reduce and simmer for 5 minutes. Reduce further and add the fish, poaching it gently for about 5-10 minutes.

Strain the fish, retaining the liquor. Pour the liquor in a saucepan and reduce; thicken with beurre manié and pour over the goujons.

SAVOURY BUTTERS

These can be served with most fish, particularly when a fish has been filleted and grilled or pan-fried.

LEMON AND PARSLEY BUTTER

100g (4oz)	butter, softened
2 tbs	very finely chopped parsley
	juice of ½ lemon
	salt and pepper to taste

Combine all the ingredients and chill.

BROWN BUTTER

100g (4oz)	butter
	juice of ½ lemon

Melt and cook the butter until it is light brown, then add the lemon juice.

MUSTARD BUTTER

100g (4oz)	butter, softened
1 tsp	Dijon mustard
	juice of ½ lemon
	salt and pepper to taste
	a little finely chopped parsley

Combine all the ingredients and chill.

WATERCRESS BUTTER

100g (4oz)	butter
75-100g (3-4oz)	watercress
	squeeze of lemon juice
	salt and pepper to taste

Carefully pick over the watercress, retaining only the perfect green leaves. Dry and chop these finely. Mix with the butter, lemon, salt and pepper. Chill.

ANCHOVY BUTTER

100g (4oz)	unsalted butter
1 tsp	gentleman's relish

Combine all the ingredients and chill.

HERB BUTTER

100g (4oz)	butter
	chopped herbs, e.g. parsley, coriander, dill, fennel or chervil

Combine all the ingredients and chill.

CRAYFISH BUTTER

	butter
	crayfish shells
	lemon juice to taste

The quantities depend on how many crayfish shells you have. Put the butter and crayfish shells in a food-processor and blend. Add a drop of lemon juice to taste, and chill.

Wine recommendation

There is one hard and fast rule when matching fish and wine; the lighter the fish, the lighter the wine. Beyond this it is all pretty simple, and yes, you can drink red wine with fish, but it will tend to need a pretty rich sauce to cope with the wine.

For the more meaty fish, such as bass the preferred route would be a decent white Burgundy, be it from the classical homes of Puligny or Meursault, through to a Pouilly Fuissé all will work well, although a new world Chardonnay would be more than acceptable.

Bream and carp tend to go best with the likes of a good Rhône white, such as a Hermitage or Châteauneuf-du-Pape, but are equally well matched with a good white Bordeaux.

Eels, and especially smoked eels and elvers, are particularly suited to fine dry Alsatian wines such as a Riesling or Pinot Blanc.

Many of the fish that tend to have an element of muddiness to their flavour will benefit from Sauvignon Blanc. Something like Pike tends to shine when drunk with a good Sancerre or New Zealand Sauvignon.

Mackerel and other oily fish will best be partnered with unoaked wines, and the list of possible wines is pretty endless, but a light, fresh rosé is often a real treat.

Trout and many similar fish like perch and grayling will go well with a Chablis, again one that is not over-powered with oak.

Salmon loves Chardonnay, be it new world or old world, but again match the sauce with the weight of the wine. Gravad lax needs an oily style of wine to complement the fish – Alsace or a good Chenin are recommended.

Shellfish such as crayfish, will again be suited to fine Chardonnay, but a good Viognier works well too.

The real key to wine and fish is to ensure that the fish and any accompanying sauce is complementary to the wine. As much as you may like good red Bordeaux, it is not the thing to drink with trout! However, you can up the power and concentration of the wine to match richer and spicier sauces.

GAME PIES

Game pies are excellent for using up leftover meat or game that is not of the best quality. Marinating the meat first will help to tenderise it and the addition of bacon, ham and vegetables will combine to make a tasty filling.

Cold game pies make an impressive centrepiece to a cold buffet and are also handy for picnics. Ingredients and quantities may be varied according to what is available and, of course, personal taste. Cooking times are approximate.

Wine recommendation

Where the game is specified, as in pheasant or duck, a rule of thumb is to keep to the recommended wines as referred to in the appropriate sections. For the more general game pies, a good Cru Beaujolais, such as a Morgan or Fleurie would go well with the raised game pie and cold game pie. A more gutsy Madiran, Cahors or South African Pinotage would be a good choice for the Hot Game Pie, while the pigeon pie could take a lighter option of a Burgundy Chorey-Les-Beaune.

PIGEON BREAST PIE

8	pigeon breasts
40g (1½oz)	butter
225g (8oz)	rump steak, cut into 2.5cm (1in) chunks
100g (4oz)	lardons
2 tbs	chopped parsley
	grated rind of 1 lemon
	stock
225g (8oz)	puff pastry
1	egg, beaten

For the marinade:

	equal quantities olive oil and
	port (about 3-4 tbs of each)
4-6	crushed juniper berries
4-6	peppercorns
1	bay leaf

Mix the marinade ingredients together and pour over the pigeon breasts. Leave for a few hours or, preferably, overnight. Dry the pigeon breasts and cut into chunks about 2.5cm (1in) square. Put the pigeon, steak and lardons in a buttered 2-pint pie dish and place a pie funnel in the centre. Sprinkle over the parsley and lemon rind, the strained marinade and sufficient stock to just cover the meat.

Top with puff pastry, glaze with a little beaten egg and bake for 10 minutes in a hot oven (200°C, 400°F, Gas Mark 6) reducing to 180°C, 350°F, Gas Mark 4 for a further 35-40 minutes.

Serves 4-6

When cutting away the breasts, retain the feet from one pigeon, scald in boiling water and place in the centre of the pie so they just stick out of the pie. A humorous touch courtesy of Mrs Beeton!

PHEASANT PIE

2	pheasants
5 tbs	butter
225g (8oz)	shortcrust pastry
570ml (1 pint)	stock
275ml (½ pint)	red or white wine
12	button onions, peeled
225g (8oz)	mushrooms
2	carrots, sliced
100g (4oz)	frozen peas
100g (4oz)	frozen broad beans
450g (1lb)	cooked new potatoes
	beaten egg or milk to glaze

Roast the pheasants in butter for 45 minutes, basting well. Cut the birds into serving pieces. Remove as many of the body bones as possible, add them to the stock and wine, and simmer for 30 minutes. Strain the liquid and thicken with a little cornflour mixed with water, if necessary.

Meanwhile cook the onions, mushrooms, carrots, peas and broad beans. Cut the potatoes in half and sauté them until they are brown.

Put the pheasant meat and all the vegetables in a deep casserole or pie dish, pour over the liquid, cover with pastry and glaze with a little milk or beaten egg. Bake in a hot oven (200°C, 400°F, Gas Mark 6) for 30 minutes.

Serves 4-6

RAISED GAME PIE

450g (1lb)	mixed cooked game, finely chopped
225g (8oz)	boneless pork, minced
100g (4oz)	pork sausagemeat
100g (4oz)	cooked ham, diced
2-3	rashers streaky bacon, diced
1	shallot, peeled and finely chopped
1 tsp	redcurrant jelly
1	pinch ground allspice
1	pinch ground bay leaves
	salt and pepper
275ml (½ pint)	reduced game stock
12g (½oz)	gelatine (1 sachet)
1 tbs	Madeira

For the hot water crust pastry:

350g (12oz)	plain flour
1	tsp salt
100g (4oz)	lard
150ml (¼ pint)	water
1	egg, beaten

Serve with a fresh fruit relish (see page 252)

Mix together the game meat, pork, sausagemeat, ham and bacon. Add the shallot, redcurrant jelly, seasonings, 2 tbs of the stock and mix well. For the pastry, sift together the flour and salt into a bowl and leave to stand in a warm place. Melt the lard in a saucepan, add the water and bring to the boil. Make a well in the flour, pour in the lard and water and mix well with a wooden spoon. Turn onto a lightly floured surface and knead until smooth. Take about two-thirds of the pastry (cover the remainder with a cloth to keep it warm) and line a 20cm (8in) loose-bottomed cake tin. Spoon in the meat filling. Brush the edges of the pastry with a little beaten egg. Roll out the remaining pastry and cover the pie, sealing the edges firmly. Use the pastry trimmings to decorate the pie, make a hole in the top for the steam to escape and glaze with the rest of the beaten egg. Bake in a hot oven (200°C, 400°F, Gas Mark 6) for 30 minutes, reducing to 180°C, 350°F, Gas Mark 4 for a further hour. If it starts to brown too much, cover with greaseproof paper. Allow to cool slightly. Dissolve the gelatine in the Madeira, add to the remaining warm stock and cool until it is just beginning to thicken.

As the pie cools, pour some of the liquid into it, using a small funnel inserted into the central hole. Allow the liquid to seep in, then add some more until it has all been absorbed in the pie.

Chill thoroughly, preferably overnight, but remove from the fridge at least 1-2 hours before serving.

Serves 8-10

COLD GAME PIE

1	thick gammon rasher, about 225g (8oz)
2	pheasants or grouse (old birds)
1	medium onion, chopped
	parsley
	salt and pepper
	pinch mace
	rind of ½ lemon
3	hard-boiled eggs
	stock to cover
100g (4oz)	mushrooms, sliced and sautéed
	forcemeat balls, fried (see pg 266)
100ml (4fl oz)	good Burgundy
25g (1oz)	gelatine (2 sachets)
225g (8oz)	shortcrust pastry (see pg 269)

Soak the gammon in water for an hour; remove and place in a casserole with the birds (which may be jointed), onion, parsley, pepper, salt (a teaspoon at this stage because the gammon will be salty), lemon rind and enough stock to cover. Stew gently on the stove or in the oven until tender. Leave to cool. Cut the flesh from the birds and cut the gammon into neat pieces, slice the hard-boiled eggs, mushrooms, forcemeat balls, previously fried, and fill the pie dish, placing a pie funnel in the centre. Put the bones and carcasses of the birds back into the stock and boil until reduced to one-third of its previous quantity. Add the wine, strain and season to taste. Dissolve the gelatine in a little water, over a pan of hot water, and add to the stock. Pour the stock into the pie dish until two-thirds full. Cover with a good shortcrust pastry and cook on the top shelf of a hot oven (200°C, 400°F, Gas Mark 6) for 10 minutes then lower the heat to 180°C, 350°F, Gas Mark 4 for a further 35-40 minutes. Cool and fill up with the remaining stock through the pie funnel, and chill.

Serves 6-8.

HOT GAME PIE

675g (1½lb)	game meat –
	retain the bones and carcasses
1	onion, sliced
1	carrot, sliced
1	stick celery, sliced
900ml(1½ pints)	stock
For the marinade:	
150ml (¼ pint)	red wine
2 tbs	olive oil
	slice of onion
1	bay leaf
	parsley
40g (1½oz)	butter
225g (8oz)	raw tongue, chopped
	beurre manié (2 tbs flour, 2 tbs butter)
	salt and pepper
6	slices bacon
100g (4oz)	sausagemeat
225g (8oz)	pastry – shortcrust or puff
1	egg, beaten

Place the bones and carcasses, onion, carrot and celery in a large saucepan with the stock, cover and simmer for about 2 hours. Strain, cool and skim off the fat.

Combine the marinade ingredients, cut the meat into chunks and marinate for a few hours or overnight, turning occasionally. Drain the meat and dry well. Brown quickly in the 40g (1½oz) butter and transfer to a casserole with the tongue and hot stock, slightly thickened with the beurre manié. Season with salt and pepper. Cover and cook in a slow oven for (150°C, 300°F, Gas Mark 2) 1½-2 hours. Cool slightly and skim off any extra fat.

Line a large pie dish with bacon and then spread over the sausagemeat. Add the game and enough stock to cover the meat. Cover with the rolled out pastry, brush with a little beaten egg and bake in a hot oven (200°C, 400°F, Gas Mark 6) for 10 minutes, reducing to 180°C, 350°F, Gas Mark 4 for a further 35-40 minutes (depending on the type of pastry used). Serves 4-6

TORTIÈRE AU CANARD (DUCK PIE)

100g (4oz)	bacon fat
1	onion, finely chopped
1	wild duck, cut into joints
1 tbs	flour
275ml (½ pint)	chicken stock
	salt and pepper
1	clove
	a little savory
	scraping of nutmeg
1 tsp	cinnamon
For the pastry:	
675g (1½lb)	shortcrust pastry (see pg 269)
1	egg, beaten or a little milk

In a pan melt the bacon fat, brown the finely chopped onion and the duck joints. Add the flour and brown. Moisten with the stock. Season with salt, pepper, clove, savory, nutmeg and cinnamon. Bring to the boil and simmer for 1½ hours on a low heat or 20 minutes in a pressure cooker.

Line a pie dish with two-thirds of the pastry and when the duck is cooked, remove the meat from the bones and put it, with the sauce (which should be quite thick) into the pie dish. Cover with the rest of the pastry and seal. Brush with a little milk or beaten egg and cook for 10 minutes at a high temperature (200°C, 400°F, Gas Mark 6) and then 30 minutes at a moderate temperature (180°C, 350°F, Gas Mark 4).

Serves 4-6

RABBIT PIE

225g (8oz)	boneless rabbit, cubed
1 tbs	Dijon mustard
6	juniper berries crushed
450g (1lb)	pork sausagemeat
225g (8oz)	streaky bacon, chopped
4 tbs	white wine
2 tbs	parsley
	salt and pepper
12g (½oz)	gelatine (1 sachet)
275ml (½ pint)	stock

For the hot water crust pastry:

350g (12oz)	plain flour
1 tsp	salt
100g (4oz)	lard
150ml (¼ pint)	water
1	egg, beaten

Put the rabbit in a bowl and coat with the mustard and crushed juniper berries. In a separate bowl, mix together the sausagemeat, bacon, white wine, parsley, salt and pepper.

For the pastry, sift together the flour and salt into a bowl and leave to stand in a warm place. Melt the lard in a saucepan, add the water and bring to the boil. Make a well in the flour, pour in the lard and water and mix well with a wooden spoon. Turn onto a lightly floured surface and knead until smooth. Take about two-thirds of the pastry (cover the remainder with a cloth to keep it warm) and line a 20cm (8in) loose-bottomed cake tin. Fill with half the sausagemeat mixture, then add the rabbit and finally the remaining sausagemeat. Roll out the rest of the pastry to make a lid, seal the edges with beaten egg and cut a cross in the centre of the lid and fold back the edges. Glaze the top with more beaten egg. Place the pie on a baking tray and cook for half an hour at (200°C, 400°F, Gas Mark 6) reducing to (180°C, 350°F, Gas Mark 4) for 1-1¼ hours. Dissolve the gelatine in a little water, over a pan of hot water, and add to the stock. When the pie is cooked, remove from the oven and as it cools pour the stock into the pie, a little at a time, through the hole in the lid. Allow to cool completely and keep, well wrapped, in a cool place until ready to serve. Serve cold with relishes

Serves 6-8

GIBLET PIE

	oil for frying
2-3	rashers streaky bacon
1	onion, chopped
1	clove garlic, crushed
1 tbs	flour
150ml (¼ pint)	game stock
1	glass red wine
450g (1lb)	giblets from gamebirds and/or chicken
	or turkey giblets, plus any
	left-over meat
2	carrots, diced
100g (4oz)	Brussels sprouts,
	cooked and sliced – optional
350g (12oz)	puff pastry
1	egg, beaten

Heat the oil in a large frying-pan and gently fry the bacon, onion and garlic. Remove with a slotted spoon. While the pan is still hot, sprinkle in about 1 tbs of flour and stir into the oil to make a roux.

Pour in the red wine and game stock, stirring all the time, to make a gravy. Add a little more stock if necessary.

Return the fried bacon, onion and garlic to the gravy, add the meat and giblets, carrots and sprouts and stir well. Pour the mixture into a pie dish and top with the puff pastry. Glaze with beaten egg and bake for 10 minutes at (200°C, 400°F, Gas Mark 6) reducing to (180°C, 350°F, Gas Mark 4) for 35-40 minutes.

Serves 4

VENISON PIE

For the marinade:

150ml (¼ pint)	red wine
1 tbs	olive oil
½	onion, chopped
1 tbs	Worcestershire sauce
1 tsp	mixed dried herbs
1 tbs	good quality redcurrant jelly

675g (1½lb)	diced venison
	oil for frying
100g (4oz)	smoked lardons
	(or smoked bacon rashers)
2-3	shallots, finely chopped
1	clove garlic, crushed
2 tbs	tomato purée
225g (8oz)	potatoes, peeled and diced
100g (4oz)	chestnut mushrooms
350g (12oz)	puff pastry
1	egg, beaten

For the marinade, melt the redcurrant jelly in a saucepan and add the remaining ingredients. Cool and pour over the venison. Cover and leave to marinate for a few hours or preferably overnight.

Remove the meat and dry well. Heat the oil in a large casserole or frying-pan and brown the venison all over. Remove, add more oil if necessary and gently fry the lardons, shallots and garlic. Return the meat to the pan and stir in half the strained marinade and the tomato purée. Bring to the boil and simmer, covered, for about 45 minutes until the meat is tender. Top up with the remaining strained marinade if necessary.

Stir in the mushrooms and cool slightly. Top with the puff pastry, glazed with a little beaten egg, and cook in a hot oven (200°C, 400°F, Gas Mark 6) for 10 minutes reducing to (180°C, 350°F, Gas Mark 4) for 35-40 minutes.

Serves 4

SAUCES, SALSAS AND RELISHES

BOB'S BREAD SAUCE

GRAVY FOR GAME

A very English sauce that suits most roast gamebirds

450ml (¾ pint)	milk
½	onion stuck with 24 cloves
12	peppercorns
1	bay leaf
50g (2 oz)	butter
75g (3oz)	fresh white breadcrumbs
	salt and pepper to taste

Pour the milk into a saucepan with the onion stuck with cloves, the peppercorns and bay leaf, warm gently, remove from the heat and leave to infuse for an hour.

Return to the heat, bring to the boil then strain, retaining the onion, and return the milk to the pan. Mix with the breadcrumbs, butter cut into small pieces and salt and pepper to taste. Stir thoroughly, adding more breadcrumbs and/or butter according to personal taste. Return the onion and cloves to the sauce, keep warm and serve in a sauce-boat.

450g (1lb)	game giblets (make up quantity with chicken giblets if necessary and add leftover game carcasses)
225g (8oz)	shin of beef
1 tbs	dripping or bacon fat
1	onion, chopped
900ml (1½ pints)	stock or water
	bouquet garni of parsley, thyme, bay leaf
	salt
8	peppercorns

Wash the giblets and dry them. Cut them into pieces with the beef and fry them gently with the onion in the dripping or bacon fat until light brown. Add about 75ml (3fl oz) of the stock or water and cook slowly, stirring occasionally, until it is reduced to a brown glaze. Add the remaining stock or water, herbs, salt, and peppercorns. Bring to the boil and then simmer, half covered, for about an hour or until reduced to 570ml (1 pint). Strain, cool and skim off the fat.

This gravy freezes well so is worth making in large quantities.

ESPAGNOLE SAUCE

1	onion, chopped
50g (2oz)	mushrooms, sliced
2	tomatoes, skinned and chopped
1	rasher bacon, chopped
50g (2oz)	butter or dripping
25g (1oz)	flour
275ml (½ pint)	brown stock
	bouquet garni
2 tbs	sherry
	salt and pepper

Melt the butter or dripping in a saucepan and fry the bacon, onion, mushrooms and tomatoes for 3-4 minutes. Add the flour and stir over a low heat. Gradually blend in the stock and bring the sauce to the boil. Add the bouquet garni and season to taste, cover the pan and simmer for 15 minutes. Remove the bouquet garni and sieve or blend in a food processor or liquidizer. Return to the pan, add the sherry and check for seasoning again. Heat for a few minutes.

SAUCE BIGARADE

A classic accompaniment for duck

2	oranges (Seville when available)
	Juice of ½ lemon
50g (2oz)	butter
25g (1oz)	flour
150ml (¼ pint)	stock (beef or game)
	salt and pepper
1 tbs	sugar
	meat juices from roasting pan – optional
	a little port or Madeira – optional

Peel the rind of the oranges as thinly as possible with a potato peeler and cut into thin shreds. Boil for 5 minutes, then drain. Melt the butter, stir in the flour and cook for a minute or two. Stir in the hot stock, whisk until smooth and simmer for 5 minutes. Add the juice from the oranges and the ½ lemon (if using Seville oranges, the lemon juice may be omitted); season with salt and pepper, add the sugar, any meat juices and a little port or Madeira, if using.

PRUNE SAUCE

BARBECUE SAUCE

A good sauce for duck

225g (8oz)	ready-to-eat pitted prunes
1 tbs	rice vinegar
3 tbs	sherry
2 tbs	tomato purée
1	dash of Tabasco
3 tbs	soy sauce
275ml (½ pint)	water

Soak the prunes in the rice vinegar overnight. Put the prunes and vinegar in a pan with the sherry, tomato purée, Tabasco, soy sauce and water. Cover and cook over a low heat for 20 minutes. Remove from the heat and blend in a food processor or liquidizer until smooth.

1	onion chopped
1	clove garlic, crushed
1 tbs	vegetable oil
1 tsp	dried mustard
1 tsp	malt vinegar
2 tbs	tomato purée
1½ tbs	brown sugar
1 tbs	soy sauce
1 tbs	Worcestershire sauce
1 tbs	lemon juice
½ tsp	ground ginger
	salt and pepper
150ml (¼ pint)	beef stock

Fry the onion in the oil until soft, add the garlic and fry for a further minute or two, then add all the remaining ingredients, mixing well. Bring to the boil and simmer for 30 minutes. Thicken with a little cornflour mixed with water, if necessary.

BROWN SAUCE

This is as good as the stock that goes into it. It can be used as a base for other sauces.

1	carrot, chopped
2	onions, chopped
100g (4oz)	fat – preferably beef or pork dripping
50g (2oz)	flour
1½ litres (2½ pints)	brown stock
1	celery stalk, chopped
1	clove garlic
1	bay leaf
3	sprigs parsley
	a little thyme
3 tbs	tomato purée

Heat the fat in a frying-pan, add the carrot and onion and cook gently for 5 minutes; add the flour and stir until it is well browned. Pour in 570ml (1 pint) of stock, then the celery, garlic and herbs, and cook, stirring, until the sauce is thick. Gradually add a further 750ml (1¼ pints) of stock.

Simmer slowly for 1½ hours, stirring occasionally and skimming off the fat until the sauce is reduced by half. Add the tomato purée and stir well. Sieve into another saucepan, add the rest of the stock and simmer for another hour, skimming the surface as necessary.

For a quicker version, melt 1½ tbs of unsalted butter and stir in 1½ tbs of flour. Cook over a low heat until the mixture is a pale brown colour. Add 450ml (¾ pint) of good brown stock or beef consommé, stir well, bring to the boil and cook for 5 minutes. Turn the heat down and simmer for 30 minutes, stirring occasionally. Skim off the fat and strain.

BROWN MUSTARD SAUCE

Serve with venison or hare

50g (2oz)	finely chopped onion
15g (½oz)	butter and 1 tbs oil melted in a saucepan, or 'degreased' roasting pan juices
225ml (8fl oz)	white wine, or 150ml (¼ pint) dry vermouth
450ml (¾ pint)	brown sauce (see page 241)
3 tbs	Dijon mustard mixed with
2 tbs	soft butter and a pinch of sugar
2 tbs	finely chopped parsley

Cook the onion slowly in butter and oil or in the juices of a roasting pan for about 10 minutes, until golden. Add the wine or vermouth and boil rapidly until it is reduced to a quarter of the original volume. Add the brown sauce and simmer for 10 minutes. Check seasoning. Remove from the heat and, just before serving, beat in the mustard and butter mixture and the parsley.

SAUCE CHASSEUR

This goes well with most types of game

50g (2oz)	finely chopped onion
25g (1oz)	butter
1 tbs	olive oil
275ml (½ pint)	tomato pulp – either fresh tomatoes, skinned, seeded and chopped or tinned tomatoes, drained, and chopped
½	clove garlic, crushed
	salt and pepper
½ tsp	dried basil or a sprig of fresh basil
150ml (¼ pint)	white wine
150ml (¼ pint)	brown sauce – see page 241
225g (8oz)	mushrooms, sliced and sautéed in butter

Sauté the onion for a minute in butter and oil, add tomatoes, garlic, salt, pepper and basil. Cover and simmer for 5 minutes; check seasoning. Add the wine and brown sauce, then add the mushrooms and simmer for a minute.

SAUCE POIVRADE

This is a popular sauce to serve with venison, particularly when the meat has been marinated. It is also used to make other sauces.

1	carrot, chopped
1	onion, chopped
3 tbs	olive oil
50g (2oz)	flour
900ml (1½ pints)	strong beef stock
1 tbs	tomato purée
	bouquet garni of bay leaf and parsley
	bones from cooked game
150ml (¼ pint)	wine vinegar
150ml (¼ pint)	strained marinade or red wine
8	peppercorns, crushed
	salt
2 tbs	butter

Brown the carrot and onion in the oil. Sprinkle over the flour and when it is brown add the stock and tomato purée. Stir well to avoid lumps and then add the bouquet garni and bones. Cover, and simmer for 2 hours. Skim off the fat. Meanwhile, mix the vinegar and marinade, if using, or red wine with the peppercorns and reduce until it is half its original volume. Add this to the strained sauce and simmer for another 30 minutes; add salt if necessary. Just before serving stir in the butter.

Variations:

1. To 450ml (¾ pint) of boiling sauce poivrade, add 150ml (¼ pint) red wine and 150ml (¼ pint) from the marinade. Cook for 30 minutes, skimming when required. Add 1 tsp sugar and cook until reduced to about half its original quantity. Before serving stir in 2 tbs butter.

2. Bring 570ml (1 pint) sauce poivrade to the boil and cook for 10 minutes. Remove from the heat and add 150ml (¼ pint) Madeira wine, 3 tbs of blanched, roasted, slivered almonds and 2 tbs small raisins, warmed in a little boiling water.

3. Mix 570ml (1 pint) hot sauce poivrade with 100g (4oz) redcurrant jelly and 100g (4oz) thick cream beaten into it just before serving. This is particularly good with venison.

4. Heat 275ml (½ pint) sauce poivrade and 275ml (½ pint) redcurrant jelly together. Stir with a whisk until there are no lumps left from the jelly. Stir in 100g (4oz) drained tinned black cherries. Good with venison, duck and goose.

FRANCATELLI'S VENISON SAUCE

2 tbs	port
225g (8oz)	good quality redcurrant jelly
	small stick of cinnamon, bruised
	thinly pared rind of lemon

Simmer together all the ingredients for 5 minutes. Strain into a hot sauce-boat.

JELLY SAUCE FOR GAME

275ml (½ pint)	good quality redcurrant jelly
275ml (½ pint)	red wine
	pinch of ginger
	pinch of cloves
	squeeze of lemon juice
1 tsp	cornflour mixed with a little water
2 tbs	brandy

Melt the jelly slowly and add the wine, mixing well with a whisk. Simmer for a few minutes until smooth, add the spices and lemon juice, thicken with the cornflour mixture, simmer for a few more minutes, then add the brandy.

Variation:

Omit the brandy and add 1 tbs of grated horseradish.

APRICOT AND BRANDY SAUCE FOR DUCK

150g (5oz)	apricot pulp
275ml (½ pint)	water
100g (4oz)	sugar
	cornflour
1 tbs	brandy or apricot brandy
	juice of ½ lemon

Put the apricot pulp through a sieve or blend in a liquidizer. Add 275 ml (½ pint) water and the sugar; simmer. Thicken with a little cornflour.

Add the brandy or apricot brandy, and lemon juice.

CUMBERLAND SAUCE

This is the best sauce for cold meat – ham, pressed beef, tongue, venison, boar's head or pork brawn

2	large oranges
4 tbs	good quality redcurrant jelly
1 heaped tsp	Dijon mustard
	a sprinkling of ground ginger – optional
70ml (2½fl oz)	medium tawny port
	salt and pepper

Cut the rind, very thinly, from the oranges with a potato peeler and slice into matchstick strips. Plunge them into boiling water and let them boil for 5 minutes. Strain and put them in a bowl with the redcurrant jelly, Dijon mustard, a little freshly milled pepper, a pinch of salt and the ground ginger, if using. Place this bowl over a saucepan of hot water, stirring all the time, until the jelly is melted and the mustard smooth. Add the port, stir and cook for another 5 minutes and serve cold (the sauce thickens as it cools).

Made in double or triple quantities, this sauce can be stored in covered jars and will keep for several weeks.

MAYONNAISE

3	egg yolks
275ml (½ pint)	olive oil
	large pinch of salt
	a little tarragon or wine vinegar,
	or lemon juice

Whisk the yolks until they start to go pale and thick, then begin whisking in the oil drop by drop. Keep adding the oil very slowly until the sauce starts to thicken, then add an occasional drop of vinegar or lemon juice (be careful not to add too much), and finish by whisking in the oil in a fine stream.

If you wish to keep it for a day or two, stir in 2 tbs of boiling water.

HOLLANDAISE SAUCE

3-4	egg yolks
1 tbs	white wine
1 tsp	water (or more for a lighter sauce)
2 tsp	lemon juice
100-150g (4-5oz)	unsalted butter
	salt and pepper

Melt the butter. Tip the egg yolks into a food processor or liquidizer and switch on. Pour the melted butter slowly through the lid or funnel. When it has thickened, add the wine, water, lemon juice, salt and pepper.

Warm the goblet or bowl of your liquidizer or food processor before starting the process.

BÉCHAMEL SAUCE

275ml (½ pint)	milk
1	slice of onion
4-6	peppercorns
1	bay leaf
40g (1½oz)	butter
2 level tbs	flour
	salt and pepper
	scraping of nutmeg – optional

Heat the milk with the onion slice, peppercorns and bay leaf. Take off the heat, cover and leave to infuse for half an hour.

In a separate saucepan melt the butter until it bubbles, but do not let it brown. Stir in the flour thoroughly and, over a low heat, gradually add the strained warm milk, stirring or whisking to smooth out any lumps. Once all the milk has been added, season to taste and simmer very gently for about 10 minutes, stirring most of the time.

When using it as a sauce with fish, substitute fish stock for some of the milk.

Variations:

To a basic béchamel sauce any of the following may be added:

1. 3 tbs tomato juice.
2. 2 tbs anchovy paste, a little more butter and a squeeze of lemon.
3. Chopped hard-boiled egg and finely chopped parsley.
4. Dijon mustard.
5. Dill.

VELOUTÉ SAUCE

If all the milk in a béchamel sauce is substituted for stock it becomes velouté. A little cream may be added.

SAUCE MOUSSELINE

3   parts hollandaise sauce to
1   part whipped cream

Fold the whipped cream into the hollandaise sauce just before serving. Season to taste.

SAUCE BRETONNE

Easier to make than mayonnaise – the taste depends a great deal on the quality and quantity of the mustard and the vinegar used.

2	egg yolks
	salt and pepper
1 tbs	Dijon mustard
1 tsp	tarragon or wine vinegar
	fresh herbs such as parsley,
	fennel, chives, tarragon, chervil or dill
75g (3oz)	very soft butter

Stir the egg yolks with the salt, pepper, mustard, vinegar and finely chopped herbs. Then, little by little, stir in the butter until the sauce is as thick as mayonnaise. This is best made just before serving, but if it loses its consistency, it can be brought back again by stirring over warm water.

This is particularly good with mackerel.

LEMON BUTTER SAUCE

DILL SAUCE

225g (8oz)	good quality unsalted butter
	juice of 1 lemon
1-2 tbs	chopped thyme or lemon thyme
	a little salt

Melt the butter gently. While still warm, pour onto the lemon juice, whisking all the time. Stir in the thyme and a little salt to taste. Serve immediately, still stirring in the sauce-boat.

1 tbs	Dijon mustard
1 tbs	castor sugar
2 tbs	white wine or tarragon vinegar
about 150ml (¼ pint)	olive oil
2-3 tbs	dill leaves

Mix together the mustard, sugar and vinegar. Add the oil, drop by drop, stirring continually as for mayonnaise, until you have a thick sauce. Add the dill leaves finely cut with scissors.

SAUCE VERTE

This is the perfect sauce for cold salmon or sea-trout.

10	leaves of fresh spinach
10	sprigs of watercress
3-4	small sprigs of parsley and tarragon
	a few chives – optional
275 ml (½ pint)	mayonnaise

Pick the leaves off the watercress, tarragon and parsley, and discard the stalks. Blanch the leaves with the spinach in boiling water for 2 minutes, then drain into a sieve, squeezing out the excess water. Chop with the chives, if using, and stir them all into the mayonnaise.

HORSERADISH SAUCE

The horseradish is best grated in a food processor to avoid too many tears!

1 tbs	grated horseradish
150ml (¼ pint)	lightly whipped cream or crème fraîche
1 tsp	lemon juice
	salt

Fold the horseradish into the cream or crème fraîche and add the lemon juice and salt. Allow to sit for about 10 minutes to mellow. If using horseradish from a jar, add about 5 tbs whipped cream to 2 tbs sauce.

SOUR CREAM & CUCUMBER SAUCE

REDCURRANT RELISH

Serve with gravad lax.

150ml (¼ pint)	sour cream
75-100g (3-4oz)	caster sugar
4 tbs	cider vinegar
	freshly ground black pepper
	lots of chopped dill
2	cucumbers, thinly sliced

Mix together the cream, sugar, vinegar, pepper and dill. Pour over the sliced cucumbers.

A good accompaniment for pheasant en croute (see page 52).

1	red onion, finely chopped
3 tbs	good quality redcurrant jelly
2-3 tbs	fresh redcurrants (or chopped fresh cranberries, according to season)
1	medium chilli, chopped

Gently warm the redcurrant jelly. Stir in the chopped onion, chilli and redcurrants or cranberries. Cook for a few minutes and serve while still crunchy.

FRESH FRUIT RELISH

MANGO SALSA

Excellent with raised game pie.

1	red onion, finely chopped
1	apple, diced
1	orange, segmented
½	lemon, segmented
	a few fresh blueberries
1	medium chilli, finely chopped
	fresh chopped parsley

Combine all the ingredients and mix well. Just before serving, add salt to taste (if salt is added too soon, the mixture will become watery).

Very good with cold game pie .

1	ripe mango
4	spring onions, finely chopped
1 tbs	olive oil
1 tbs	parsley chopped

Peel the mango and remove the flesh from the stone. Dice fairly finely and add the remaining ingredients. Mix, cover and leave for an hour to allow the flavours to mingle.

SALSA VERDE   TOMATO SALSA

Goes well with duck or fish.

2	cloves garlic, chopped
	salt
4	anchovy fillets, drained, rinsed in milk and chopped – optional
3 tbs	each of parsley, mint and basil
1-2 tbs	capers, rinsed and chopped
70ml (2½fl oz)	extra virgin olive oil
2 tbs	fresh lime juice
	a dash of green Tabasco
3	spring onions, chopped

Mash the garlic with the salt until it becomes a paste. Stir in all the other ingredients and leave for about an hour to allow the flavours to mix together.

This sauce will keep for a few days with a thin layer of olive oil on top.

Vary quantities according to personal taste.

225g (8oz)	ripe tomatoes, roughly chopped
2	cloves garlic, crushed
1	red pepper, deseeded and chopped
1	red onion, chopped
1	medium chilli, deseeded and chopped
	a bunch of fresh coriander, chopped
2-3 tbs	olive oil
	a squeeze of lemon juice
	salt and pepper to taste

Combine all the ingredients and mix well.

For a fresher tasting salsa, substitute coriander with mint.

VEGETABLES AND OTHER ACCOMPANIMENTS

GAME CHIPS

A classic accompaniment to roast pheasant and partridge.

good quality potatoes, very thinly sliced

oil for cooking

Peel the potatoes and slice as thinly as possible with a food processor, mandolin or potato peeler. Soak in a large bowl of cold water for an hour to remove the starch; stir them around so they don't stick together. Drain and dry carefully in a clean tea towel.

Heat the oil until a cube of bread sizzles in it, then fry the slices of potato a few at a time until they come to the top; remove. When they are all cooked, turn up the heat and fry in larger batches until they are golden brown. Keep pushing them around so they don't stick together. Drain on paper towels. They will stay quite crisp in a warm oven on a paper towel, uncovered.

Alternatively buy good quality crisps.

BRAISED SPROUTS WITH CHESTNUTS

675g (1½lb)	Brussels sprouts
450g (1lb)	chestnuts
50-75g (2-3oz)	butter
450ml (¾ pint)	brown stock or 275ml (½ pint) tinned consommé and 150ml (¼ pint) water
	salt and pepper

Blanch the Brussels sprouts in a large pot of boiling water and simmer, uncovered, for 6 minutes. Drain. Place the chestnuts in a casserole with 25g (1oz) of the butter and cover with stock; add more water if necessary. Bring to a simmer, cover, and place in a moderately slow oven (170°C, 325°F, Gas Mark 3) for ¾-1 hour or until tender. The liquid should be reduced to a syrup, but if not, boil it down and pour it back over the chestnuts. Roll them around to coat them. Place the sprouts and chestnuts in layers in a buttered casserole, add salt and pepper, and pour over the remaining butter, melted.

Cover tightly, bring to sizzle on top of the cooker, and place in a moderate oven (180°C, 350°F, Gas Mark 4) for 20 minutes.

SAUTÉED SPROUTS WITH BACON & CHESTNUTS

	butter or oil for frying
2	rashers streaky bacon, chopped
450g (1lb)	small Brussels sprouts
225g (8oz)	cooked chestnuts
	salt and pepper to taste

Steam or parboil the sprouts for about 5 minutes or until just tender. Melt the butter or oil in a frying-pan and add the bacon. Fry until golden then add the sprouts and chestnuts and sauté for 5-10 minutes. Season to taste.

RED CABBAGE WITH APPLES AND ONIONS

Red cabbage is a classic accompaniment to game, especially venison and goose.

1	red cabbage, about 900g (2lb)
2	onions, sliced
3	large cooking apples, peeled, cored and sliced
1	clove garlic, crushed – optional
50g (2oz)	brown sugar
	salt and pepper
¼ tsp	each of powdered nutmeg, allspice, cinnamon and thyme
275 ml (½ pint)	red wine or 3 tbs port
2 tbs	wine vinegar

Remove the outer leaves of the cabbage, cut the remainder into quarters and remove the hard white stalk. Slice thinly. Place in a casserole in layers with the onion, apple, garlic, if using, sugar, salt, pepper and spices. Add wine or port and vinegar. Place in a slow oven (150°C, 300°F, Gas Mark 2) for at least 3 hours.

CHESTNUT PURÉE

CHESTNUT CROQUETTES

A wonderful accompaniment for game.

450g (1lb)	peeled chestnuts
	½ milk and ½ stock or water
	sufficient to cover the chestnuts
40g (1½oz)	butter
1	onion, finely chopped
	salt and pepper
6 tbs	cream

Pour the milk and stock or water over the chestnuts to cover, bring to the boil and simmer for about 20 minutes. Melt 25g (1oz) of the butter, add the onion and cook gently, not letting it brown, until it is tender.

Drain the chestnuts, add the onion, mash them together and put the mixture through a mouli or blend in a food processor or liquidizer. Add plenty of salt and pepper and whisk in the remaining butter and cream. Reheat gently.

15g (½oz)	butter
2	shallots, chopped
225g (8oz)	chestnut purée – this may be tinned
	salt and pepper
2	eggs
	seasoned flour
	dried white breadcrumbs
	deep fat for frying

Melt the butter and fry the shallots lightly; do not let them brown. Mix them with the chestnut purée, salt and pepper and 1 egg, beaten. Shape into small balls, dust with seasoned flour, dip in the remaining egg, beaten, roll in breadcrumbs and fry until golden in deep fat.

CURRIED CAULIFLOWER

1	small onion, chopped
	ghee or butter
2 tsp	ground curry spices
1	cauliflower
	salt and pepper

Fry the chopped onion in ghee or butter until soft – add the ground curry spices. Fry for 2-3 minutes then add the coarsely chopped raw cauliflower. Turn gently until tender. Season to taste and add a little water if necessary.

225g (8oz) diced boiled potatoes may be added to this dish.

BRAISED CELERY

2	celery hearts, topped, tailed
	and quartered
	sufficient chicken or vegetable stock
	to cover the celery

Place the celery hearts in a shallow dish and pour over the stock. Cover with tin foil, cook in a preheated oven set at (170°C, 325°F, Gas Mark 3) for 1½-2 hours until tender.

Tinned celery hearts work well, too. Cook in the same way for about half an hour.

PURÉE OF LENTILS

450g (1lb)	dried lentils
1.2 litres (2 pints)	stock (game or chicken)
100g (4oz)	smoked sausage or salt pork
2	sprigs parsley
2	small onions, sliced
1	clove garlic, whole
1	bouquet garni
	salt and pepper
25g (1oz)	butter – optional
150ml (¼ pint)	double cream – optional

Wash the lentils and drain. Place in a saucepan, cover with stock, add the sausage or pork, parsley, onion, garlic and bouquet garni. Bring slowly to the boil and simmer for about 1½ hours. Add boiling water if it becomes too thick. When the lentils are soft, remove the bouquet garni and the garlic clove and put the rest of the mixture through a sieve or liquidize them. Put back on the heat and whip in the butter and cream, if using, and season to taste.

ITALIAN POTATOES

Suitable for most game, especially wild duck.

675g (1½lb)	mashed potatoes
	juice and grated rind of 2 oranges
40g (1½oz)	butter

Mix the orange juice, half the orange rind and 25g (1oz) of butter with the mashed potatoes. Place in an ovenproof dish, dot with the rest of the butter and sprinkle with the remaining rind. Place in a moderate oven (180°C, 350°F, Gas Mark 4) until brown – about 15 minutes.

OVEN BROWN POTATOES

Good with most roasts and casseroles.

900g (2lb)	potatoes
	salt
40g (1½oz)	butter
2 tbs	olive oil

Peel the potatoes and cut into 2cm (¾ in) cubes. Put them in a pan, cover with cold water, add salt and bring to the boil. Drain. Melt the butter and oil in a casserole or small roasting pan large enough for the potatoes not to crowd each other. Put the potatoes in the pan, roll around in the fat so they are coated all over, and place in a moderate oven (180°C, 350°F, Gas Mark 4) for about ¾-1 hour. Turn them occasionally. They should be golden brown and quite crispy.

PURÉE OF CELERIAC AND POTATOES

1	large celeriac
100g (4oz)	butter
	the weight of the celeriac in potatoes
	salt and pepper
2 tbs	cream

Peel and cut the celeriac into 2.5 cm (1in) cubes. Blanch in boiling water for 10 minutes, drain and add 75g (3oz) of the butter, then cover and cook gently for 20 minutes. Sieve, put through a mouli or liquidize.

Peel and boil the potatoes, sieve or mash them well, and add to the celeriac. Season with salt and pepper and whisk in the remaining butter and cream.

This works well using swede or carrot instead of the celeriac.

MEDLEY OF ROOT VEGETABLES

Any root vegetable can be used in this dish and quantities can be altered according to personal choice.

1	swede
2-3	parsnips
1-2	turnips
2-3	carrots
225g (½ lb)	potatoes, halved
2-3	red onions
6-8	cloves garlic
2-3	sprigs rosemary, chopped
5-6 tbs	olive oil
	sea salt and freshly ground black pepper

Peel the swede, parsnips, turnips and carrots and cut into even-sized chunks – about 2.5cm (1in). Peel the potatoes and cut in half (quarters if very large) and peel and quarter the onions. Peel the garlic and leave whole.

Put all the vegetables into a bowl, pour over the olive oil, sprinkle in the rosemary and mix well. Leave for a few hours before cooking.

Place in a large roasting tin, sprinkle with salt and pepper and roast at (200°C, 400°F, Gas Mark 6) for ¾-1 hour, turning over the vegetables once, until cooked through.

A GENERAL MARINADE FOR GAME

The purpose of marinating game is to increase the flavour and to make it more tender. The acid ingredients are what help to break down the flesh, so if you think the meat might be tough, reduce the wine and add more wine vinegar or lemon juice. How long to marinate is a matter of personal choice.

4-6 tbs	olive oil
½ bottle	red wine
1	onion, sliced
3	sprigs parsley
1	bay leaf
8	peppercorns, crushed
¼ tsp	thyme

Optional:

3 tbs	wine vinegar or 3 tbs brandy
2	carrots, sliced
3	cloves
6	juniper berries, crushed
1	clove garlic, crushed

Combine all the ingredients and mix well.

A SIMPLE MARINADE FOR GAMEBIRDS

equal quantities of olive oil and port

equal quantities of crushed juniper berries and peppercorns

Combine all the ingredients and mix well.

COURT BOUILLON
(FOR A LARGE FISH)

3 litres (5½ pints)	water
1 litre (1¾ pints)	white wine
275ml (½ pint)	wine vinegar
3	onions, stuck with 3 cloves in each
3	carrots
2	large celery stalks
2	bay leaves
5-6	large sprigs of parsley
1 tbs	salt

Combine the ingredients and use according to recipe.

BASIC GAME STOCK

FISH STOCK

1	chicken carcass
	additional bones from game
	eg pheasant carcass, venison bones
1	onion, sliced
1	carrot, sliced
6	peppercorns
1	bay leaf
	salt
	a few sprigs fresh thyme
	water

Put all the ingredients into a large saucepan and add sufficient water to cover.

Bring to the boil and simmer, partly covered, for about 1½ hours. Strain, skim and use according to individual recipe.

A useful base for fish soups and sauces.

450g (1lb)	raw fish head and bones
1	leek, chopped
1	stalk celery, chopped
1	large onion, chopped
1	clove garlic
2 tsp	salt
12	peppercorns
1	bay leaf
	bunch of parsley with stalks
1½ litres (2½ pints)	water

Place all the ingredients in a large saucepan, bring to the boil and simmer for about half an hour. Strain and use according to individual recipe.

FRIED BREADCRUMBS

FRIED BREADCRUMBS
WITH A DIFFERENCE

A traditional accompaniment to roast gamebirds.

50g (2oz)	clarified butter
40g (1½oz)	fresh breadcrumbs

Melt the butter - if it is not clarified, skim it well.

Add the breadcrumbs and stir over a moderate heat until they are pale brown.

A variation on a theme.

50g (2oz)	butter or bacon fat
50g (2oz)	bacon or ham, finely chopped
50g (2oz)	mushrooms, finely chopped
40g (1½oz)	breadcrumbs

Melt the butter or fat, fry the bacon or ham until it starts to brown (less fat is needed if using streaky bacon), then stir in the mushrooms. Cook for a minute or two, then add the breadcrumbs. Continue stirring over a moderate heat until the breadcrumbs are golden.

CROUTONS

bread

olive oil and butter for frying

Simply fry slices of bread in a mixture of hot oil and butter until golden. Cut into triangles and place around a serving dish.

For smaller croutons, cut bread into cubes and deep-fry until golden.

STUFFING FOR PHEASANT

WALNUT STUFFING

2	medium apples, peeled, cored and diced
2	medium onions, chopped
4	sticks celery, chopped
25g (1oz)	softened butter
½ tsp	marjoram or thyme
	a grate of nutmeg

Combine all the ingredients and mix well.

Ideal for duck or goose.

50g (2oz)	butter
100g (4oz)	chopped onion
1	large clove garlic, crushed
2	large eating apples, peeled, cored and diced
350g (12oz)	belly of pork, minced
100g (4oz)	breadcrumbs
50g (2oz)	walnuts, chopped
2 tsp	honey
1	large egg, beaten
1 tbs	chopped parsley
	salt and pepper
	liver from the bird – optional

Melt the butter and gently fry the onion, garlic, apples and pork for about 15 minutes. Mix with the other ingredients. Add the chopped liver of the bird, if using.

CRANBERRY STUFFING

For goose or a boned roast of venison.

25g (1oz)	suet, finely chopped
450g (1lb)	cranberries, chopped
350g (12oz)	sugar
150g (5oz)	breadcrumbs
1 tbs	grated orange rind
	salt and pepper

Fry the suet until it is crisp. Add the cranberries and sprinkle with the sugar. Stir until the berries are transparent. Add the breadcrumbs, orange rind, salt and pepper. Mix well.

FORCEMEAT BALLS

These go well with roasts and casseroles.

100g (4oz)	white breadcrumbs
40g (1½oz)	suet or melted butter
1 tbs	chopped parsley
1 tbs	chopped mixed herbs or ½ tbs thyme
	salt and pepper
1	egg, beaten

Mix all the ingredients together and roll into small balls. Cook with the meat in a roasting tin or fry in olive oil until golden.

HERB DUMPLINGS
Hugh Fearnley-Whittingstall

Excellent with jugged hare (see page 154).

100g (4oz)	self-raising flour
100g (4oz)	fresh white breadcrumbs
100g (4oz)	suet
2	eggs
	salt and pepper
	small bunch of chives, finely chopped
	small bunch of wild chervil, finely chopped
	a dozen young nettle leaves, finely chopped or substitute equivalent of parsley and thyme

Thoroughly mix the flour, breadcrumbs, suet, chopped herbs and leaves, salt and pepper in a large mixing bowl. Make a well in the middle. Beat the eggs lightly with a fork and pour three-quarters into the well. Mix with a fork bringing the dry ingredients into the centre and mixing to form a dough. Work with your hands until smooth, adding more beaten egg if necessary. Do not over-knead.

Divide the dough into 12 dumplings. Cook on top of a casserole or jugged hare, with the lid on, for the final 25 minutes of cooking time. Arrange them, if possible, so they do not touch.

WALDORF SALAD

An American classic that works well with game.

100g (4oz)	diced celery
100g (4oz)	diced apple, peeled or unpeeled
100g (4oz)	grapes, halved and pipped – optional
50g (2oz)	walnuts or pecan nuts
	French dressing with
	a little mayonnaise added

Mix together the celery, apple, nuts and grapes, if using. Pour over the dressing.

ORANGE AND WATERCRESS SALAD

A good choice with roast wild duck.

4	bunches watercress
2	oranges

For the French dressing:

4 tbs	olive oil
1 tbs	vinegar or lemon and vinegar mixed
	salt and pepper

Wash and pick over the watercress. Dry well. Peel the oranges and cut into thin segments, discarding pith and skin. Place the watercress in a salad bowl with the orange segments, combine the dressing ingredients and pour over the salad.
Toss and serve.

ROWANBERRY JELLY

BASIC SHORTCRUST PASTRY

A very good accompaniment, especially for venison.

rowanberries

sugar

(use 450g/1lb sugar to

570ml/1 pint of rowanberry juice)

Pick the berries from the stalks – the berries must be just ripe, firm and dry. Put them in a large pan, cover with water and boil until they are soft, about 10-15 minutes. Mash them lightly with a potato masher and strain them through a jelly bag.

Mix the juice with the appropriate amount of sugar, bring slowly to the boil, stirring until the sugar has melted, then increase the heat and boil rapidly until it jells. This can take anything from 20-40 minutes. Pour into pots. The jelly is better for having been left for several months.

A couple of cooking apples or some crab-apples can enhance the flavour and helps the jelly to set.

175g (6oz)	flour
	salt
40g (1½oz)	butter, at room temperature
40g (1½oz)	lard, at room temperature
	cold water to mix

Sift the flour and a pinch of salt into a large mixing bowl. Add the butter and lard in pieces and rub into the flour until the mixture resembles fine breadcrumbs. Stir in enough cold water to bring the mixture together. Add water a little at a time until the dough forms a smooth ball. Rest the pastry in the refrigerator for ½ an hour, wrapped in foil or cling film, then it is ready for use. Follow recipe instructions.

PREPARING GAME

The prospect of a gamebird in the feather or a freshly shot rabbit can be a daunting one for anyone who is used to buying meat ready prepared. But, like most things in life, it really isn't that difficult once you know how.

There are a few basic rules to preparing game which, once learnt, will never be forgotten and the task will not seem nearly as overwhelming a second time. A sharp knife and a good pair of poultry shears will make the job a lot easier.

Alternatively take your gamebird to a friendly butcher or poulterer and he will prepare it for the oven for a small cost. *We have not covered venison as this requires expert butchering skills.*

HANGING GAME

Meat is hung in order to improve both its flavour and its texture. How long to hang or, indeed, whether to hang at all is very much a matter of personal choice and the age of the bird will also be a factor (see section on Ageing gamebirds, page 274). What is most important is where and how to hang.

Whether using a garage, outhouse or shed, good ventilation and cool conditions are vital. The air must be able to circulate round the bird or piece of meat, so do not choose a small, cramped place. Ideally the temperature should not rise above 55°F but this is not always possible to achieve. If in doubt, hang for a shorter period of time.

Of equal importance is that the area is kept totally free from flies and other animals, which can provide a health risk. A fly screen is the best way to ensure this; these can be bought from specialist suppliers or can be made from a lightweight frame fitted with some fine gauze or net curtain material. The birds must never touch the screen.

Gamebirds are hung by the neck before plucking or drawing takes place; if you have a brace, separate them so the air can circulate freely round both birds.

Hare should be hung by the feet before skinning or paunching (gutting). The blood can be collected in a bowl placed under the hare if it is required for the recipe. Rabbit must be paunched as soon after shooting as possible and then hung by the feet, if desired. Venison should be hung in the same way as beef.

HOW LONG TO HANG GAME

The following is an approximate guide only. Early in the season when the birds are young, there may be no need to hang or possibly just for a day or two in the case of pheasant and not at all for partridge and grouse. Remember the grouse season opens on August 12 so conditions can be very warm, in which case eat any birds bagged fairly quickly. On the other hand in the cold, winter months a pheasant will be fine if hung for anything up to 3 weeks.

PHEASANT – up to 10 days
PARTRIDGE – 3-5 days
GROUSE – 2-4 days
WOODCOCK AND SNIPE – 5-10 days

PIGEON – no need to hang
WILD DUCK – 1-2 days
WILD GOOSE – up to 3 weeks
RABBIT – 3-4 days
HARE – 1-2 weeks
VENISON – up to 2 weeks

HOW TO PLUCK GAMEBIRDS

It is a lot easier to pluck outdoors since it doesn't matter where the feathers and down go. Otherwise use as large and deep a box or dustbin as possible in the hope that it will catch most of the feathers.

Pheasants are probably the hardest gamebirds to pluck, so if you can pluck a pheasant, you can pluck anything. Cut off the wings at the first joint on small birds and on badly shot birds, cut them off completely. Pull the head back and down under its back to make the breast feathers stand up, then pluck them, one at a time, taking great care not to tear the skin. The thigh feathers should be plucked out individually too, but the remainder can come out by the handful. Pluck against the way the feathers lie, using your thumb against your bent first finger. Try all the time to avoid tearing the skin: sometimes when the skin is torn you will have to pluck around it, pulling the feathers out the way they grow. Use tweezers for the pin feathers.

Singeing will get rid of hairs or down, but be careful not to burn the skin. Run a lit taper over the bird, or pass the bird over a dish of lit methylated spirits.

In America the custom is to dip feathered gamebirds in hot paraffin wax, allow them to cool and just pull off the feathers. *Never draw birds before plucking as they will become very difficult to handle.*

HOW TO DRAW (CLEAN)

Cut off the head so that the neck is as long as possible (except for woodcock and snipe when the head can be left on). Pull back the skin and cut the neck close to the body.

Make an incision just above the vent and remove the entrails (intestines, heart, liver, gizzard and gall bladder) gently but completely; by taking hold of the gizzard and pulling, most of the contents will come with it. If you have not removed the vent, cut the intestine close to it. Feel around to make sure there is nothing left. Try to ease out the crop without breaking it, but if it is punctured, clean out the cavity and pull out the skin of the crop.

Wipe well with a clean damp cloth. Retain the liver, heart and gizzard. Be careful to discard the gall bladder without puncturing it. If the liver has any discoloration cut that out immediately. If you wish to remove the tendons from the legs, cut carefully around the skin just at the joint where the scaly bit begins, being careful not to cut the tendons; snap the joint and pull away – the tendons should come, but if not force a skewer under them and pull them out separately.

HOW TO TRUSS

The point of trussing a bird is to keep it as compact as possible: the legs and wings don't dry out, it looks more attractive and is easier to carve, though it is not essential and birds cook quicker if they are not trussed. Use either a trussing needle and thick thread, wooden cocktail sticks or skewers and string to close the hole near the vent.

If the legs will fit, place the ends into the vent or into a slit made in that region. With a perfect bird you should be able to fold the skin of the neck down over the back and secure it with the wing tips which you bend backwards, but this isn't always possible and you will have to improvise with some of the above-mentioned equipment.

For woodcock and snipe: twist the head round and, using the beak as a skewer, pass it under the wings, through the legs and into the body.

JOINTING

Gamebirds: To halve birds, cut along the breastbone with a sharp knife then cut through with poultry shears and continue all the way round to the backbone which can be left on one half or removed. Spatchcocked gamebirds are cut down the backbone, opened up and pressed flat, usually for grilling. They can be held open by two skewers.

Gamebirds are quartered in the same way as chickens by keeping the breast and wing on one joint and the leg – both thigh and drumstick – on the other.

Rabbit and hare: Remove the legs and leave whole, except for larger animals when the hind legs can be cut in half at the joint. Discard the head and cut the back into portions of a similar size or leave whole if a saddle is required.

REMOVING THE BREAST ONLY

Many people, particularly if they have a glut of pheasant or pigeon, use the breast meat only. In this case there is no need to pluck or draw, simply cut the skin across the breastbone and pull off the skin and feathers together. Then cut along the breastbone and remove the meat on either side.

Meat from the rest of the bird can be cut roughly and used in casseroles or to make stock.

PAUNCHING AND SKINNING RABBIT AND HARE

Always paunch (gut) rabbit as soon as possible. Hare can be hung first, then paunched. Make a slit the length of the stomach and gently pull out the intestines. The kidneys and liver can be pulled out separately and kept for use in pâtés or stuffings.

To remove the skin: sever all four legs at the first joint. Cut through the skin around the hind legs, just below the tail. Peel the skin down the hind legs as if taking off a stocking. Tie the hind legs together and hang on a hook, then pull the skin down over the body and forelegs. Cut off the head. Rinse the meat in cold water and dry with paper towels.

FREEZING GAME

Only freeze the best and do not overhang it. Game should not be frozen in the feather or the fur unless you have a specific freezer for this purpose. Wrap the game very well, padding any broken bones with foil so they do not pierce the bag. Special freezer bags should always be used and the air should be extracted (suck it out with a straw) before sealing well. Good quality game, properly sealed and wrapped, will keep for up to 9 months.

Always defrost game slowly at room temperature or in a refrigerator. If a bird appears to be slightly dried by freezer burn after it has thawed, soak it in milk or single cream for 2-3 hours. This should make the bird more tender and bring back the original flavour.

PREPARING FISH

Once caught, fish should be cleaned and eaten as soon as possible. If they must be stored, keep in the coldest part of the fridge – this applies to shop-bought fish too.

If your fish has been caught in muddy water, it can be soaked in a mixture of 1 litre of fresh water to 2 tbs of wine vinegar and 1 tsp salt, changing the water as necessary.

As with game, preparing fish is just a matter of practice and having the right tools for the job – a sharp, thin-bladed knife is essential, particularly for filleting, and a fish scaler is useful though a blunt knife will do.

TO DESCALE AND CLEAN

To descale, hold the fish by the tail under cold running water and scrape towards the head with a fish scaler or blunt knife, in the opposite way to which the scales lie.

To clean, remove the fins and make a cut right along the belly of the fish and pull out the guts. Wash well in cold water and pat dry with kitchen towels.

FILLETING FISH

Cut around the back of the head with a sharp, thin-bladed, flexible knife. Turn the blade of the knife towards the tail and start to cut away the fillet, keeping the blade as flat against the bones as possible. As soon as the whole blade of the knife is under the fillet, rest your other hand on top of the fish and cut the fillet away in one clean sweep, down towards the tail. Turn the fish over and repeat on the other side.

TO BONE FISH

After the fish has been cleaned, run your thumb along the backbone, very firmly, several times until the bone begins to loosen. Turn over, ease the backbone out with as many smaller bones attached as possible. Alternatively the bone can just be cut away with a sharp knife but a lot of the flesh can be lost in this way.

SMOKING FISH

Smoked fish has a wonderful flavour and is an excellent way of preparing most varieties of fish. Hot smoking consists of simply cooking the fish in a smoke-filled place. Cold smoking, where the smoke needs to be kept going at a lower temperature over a longer period, is harder to achieve at home. Fish can be smoked whole, when cleaned, or as fillets. There are a number of home-smokers on the market from the well-known Abu to the simple foil envelope that can be used on an open fire with great ease.

It is advisable to soak the fish in brine first for about an hour and then let it air dry for a while before putting it in the smoker. Small trout and grayling are particularly good this way. A selection of home-smokers are available from Farlows of Pall Mall, tel 0207 839 2423.

FREEZING FISH

Fish is better when frozen whole and it should be put in the deep-freeze as soon after catching as possible. Simply clean the fish – except in the case of salmon and sea-trout where the gut is usually empty so they can be cleaned after thawing – and wrap well.

TO TELL THE AGE OF GAME

Before deciding how to cook a gamebird or whether or not to hang it, it is useful to know how old it is. Countrymen and women have developed their own theories on this subject over the years and experience certainly counts for a lot here. One method that seems to be more reliable than others has become known as the *Bursa Test*. All young gamebirds have a small, blind-ended passage opening on the upper side of the vent. This passage, known as the bursa, is believed to play some part in disease control. In all species it becomes much reduced and may close completely when the bird reaches sexual maturity, so the presence of a 'normal' bursa is a sure sign of a young bird. The test can be applied to both the cock and the hen bird relatively easily. *Take a matchstick which is burnt at one end so that it is narrow but not too sharp. Insert the matchstick into the bursa (the site of the opening is often marked by a slight bump) and you will be able to gauge the age of your bird. In young pheasants the depth of the bursa will be approximately 2.5cm (1in) – slightly less in smaller gamebirds – but this shortens as the bird matures and in old birds it may be closed completely.*

PHEASANT

If using the *Bursa Test* the depth of the bursa will be about 2.5cm (1in) in young birds. Another method is to look at the spurs on the bird's legs. Early in the season young cocks may be separated from old by their blunt and relatively short spurs. It is generally assumed that the longer the spurs, the older the bird, but later in the season the spurs of early-hatched young pheasants can be as long and as sharply pointed as some old birds, so this is not always a reliable test.

GREY PARTRIDGE

The *Bursa Test* can be applied to ascertain the age of a grey partridge but the matchstick will only go in about 1cm (½in) on a young bird. Sometimes it is possible to guess the age by the bird's appearance. In September and early October the familiar dark beak, yellowish legs and relatively soft bones of the young birds will readily differentiate them from the grey-beaked, grey-legged, hard-boned adults. Later in the season, however, the simple flight feathers test is to be recommended. Examine the two outer primary or flight feathers. The pointed, lance-shaped tips of these feathers distinguish the young bird from the old, which has blunt-ended outer primaries. In September a few partridges in their second year may not have moulted these sharply pointed primaries of the juvenile plumage, but the feathers will be faded and abraded to such an extent that the bird will be easily recognised as old.

RED-LEGGED PARTRIDGE

In a red-legged partridge the bursa is about the same as for the grey. Alternatively, examine the two outer primaries – not for shape but for colour markings. The young bird has these two flight feathers tipped with a cream colour; sometimes other primaries not yet moulted will also show this cream colouration.

GROUSE

The *Bursa Test* applies again. With a young grouse the matchstick can be inserted about 1cm (½in). An alternative, but not so reliable, test is to compare the two outer primary feathers with the other feathers. If they are all of a kind with rounded tips, then it is an old bird. If the tips of the two outermost feathers are pointed and clearly differ in shape from the others, it will be a young bird. However a bird of the previous year, which has not yet moulted these two primaries, will exhibit the same feathers, except that the two primaries will look tattered and faded in colour.

Another guide is that the adult grouse shed their toenails between July and September. When a nail is seen in the process of becoming detached, it is a sure sign of an old bird. A transverse ridge or scar across the top of the nail, where the old nail was attached, may persist for a month or more after it has been shed and so is indicative of an old bird.

Some favour the traditional method of breaking the lower beak or crushing the skull with the thumb. If they break easily, it is said to indicate a young bird, but this can be misleading and unreliable.

WOODCOCK AND SNIPE

Young birds have ragged feather ends on the two outer primary feathers, whereas on older birds they are smooth.

PIGEON

A young pigeon doesn't have the distinctive white collar – this develops in the mature bird.

RABBIT

A young rabbit should have soft ears, which are easily torn, and sharp teeth and claws. They should be plump with smooth fur – a rabbit becomes grey with age.

DUCK

It is not easy to tell the age of duck – some say the webbing of the feet of a young duck can be torn more easily. In mallard the feet of young duck are said to be pinker in colour and the bills brighter than in older birds.

There is little deterioration in the quality of the meat in older birds, so being able to tell the age is not so important.

GEESE

In general, birds of the year tend to lack the strong, clear cut markings of the adult, but where the adult is plain on the breast and the belly, there is often a fine soft-edged speckling in the juvenile.

One feature which is distinctive for part of the winter is the notch in the tail feather of the juvenile where the downy feather was once attached. The notch is a 'V', about 3mm (⅛in) deep and wide. It must not be confused with a broken tail feather: since moulting occurs progressively during the winter there may be only one juvenile feather to be seen. After the loss of this one, other characteristics have to be assessed. As the season progresses, ageing becomes less certain.

Characteristics

	JUVENILE	ADULT
PINK-FOOTED GOOSE		
Bill:	blotchy flesh colour	banded pink on black
Head:	pale and brownish	dark blackish tint
Breast and belly:	speckled	plain
Legs:	pale pink	pink
GREYLAG GOOSE		
Bill:	pale orange	orange
Body:	markings soft	markings distinct
Breast and belly:	few speckles	distinct spots if present
Legs:	greyish pink	pink
WHITE-FRONTED GOOSE		
Bill: white forehead absent but developing later		white forehead
Belly: no black bands but developing later		variable black bands present
Legs: paler and pinker than adult		orange
CANADA GOOSE		
Cheek patch: greyer than adult		white
Body: markings similar to adult		fewer soft brown feathers

Glossary of cooking terms

Bain-marie
A tin or dish half-filled with hot water in which a terrine or other receptacle is slowly cooked; also used to keep sauces warm.

Bard
This is simply covering the meat with slices of pork fat or streaky bacon, making sure that the breastbone and thigh bones are particularly covered. Tie these on with string. You may wish to remove the fat several minutes before the bird is cooked in order to allow it to become brown.

Baste
To spoon the juices over meat to keep it moist.

Beurre manié
A paste of kneaded butter and flour (approximately 25g (1oz) flour to 20g (¾oz)butter. used for thickening gravies, soups and sauces. Add little pieces of the paste to the boiling liquid and stir until it has thickened.

Bouquet garni
A small bunch of herbs tied together or put in a small muslin bag so that they may be easily removed before serving. It is used for flavouring liquids and food cooked in liquids and is normally composed of a bay leaf, parsley and thyme, though other herbs may be included.

Braise
Cook food which you have normally browned first, then add a layer of boiling liquid and simmer in a tightly covered pot.

Brown
Quickly fry meat so that the outside is brown without the inside being cooked. The meat must be completely dry or sprinkled with flour, and it will not brown if there are too many pieces in the pan. The pieces should not be touching each other.

Civet
A stew of game (normally furred rather than feathered game).

Clarified butter
Butter that has been melted until it just froths, is then cooled and filtered through a fine cloth or coffee filter.

Croutons
Slices of bread with their crusts trimmed, cut into various shapes and fried in oil or butter.

Dice
Cut into small cubes.

Dredge
Cover lightly by sprinkling or rolling the food in flour or whatever else the recipe suggests.

Green peppercorns
Tinned peppercorns in their soft undried state.

Lard
1. Cooking fat
2. Inserting strips of pork fat or bacon into very lean meat to give it moisture while cooking. Use a larding needle or make a slit in the meat and push the strips in with any implement. They should be placed about 2.5cm (1in) apart.

Lardons
Cubes of bacon – smoked or unsmoked.

Marinade
A highly seasoned mixture usually comprising wine, lemon juice or vinegar, olive oil, vegetables, herbs and seasoning. Meat is left to stand in this to increase its flavour and to make it more tender.

Marinate
To put meat in a marinade.

Mouli
A food mill for making purées, especially useful when a liquidizer will destroy the required texture.

Pepper
Every recipe that calls for pepper means freshly ground black peppercorns from a peppermill.

Reduce
Evaporate a liquid by boiling it uncovered over a high heat until you have the quantity you wish. This increases the flavour.

Roux
A blend of butter and flour, mixed together over a low heat. It is capable of absorbing six times its own weight when cooked.

Salmis
A dish in which the bird has been partially roasted, carved and served in a rich sauce.

Sauté
To fry gently in a little butter or oil.

Simmer
To cook just under boiling point with bubbles only at the sides of the pan.

Steam
To cook in steam over a pan of boiling water.

Trivet
A rack which will support game, breast down, for roasting. They are usually adjustable.

SHOOTING SEASONS & COOKING GUIDE

TYPE OF GAME	Nº OF SERVINGS	SHOOTING SEASONS (DATES INCLUSIVE)	AVERAGE WEIGHT	APPROX. ROASTING TIMES/ TEMPERATURES
DUCK		Below high tide mark September 1-February 20, elsewhere September 1-January 31		
Mallard	2-3 servings		1.1-1.3kg (2½-3lb)	Very hot oven 230°C, 450°F, Gas Mark 8 for 20-30 minutes
Teal	1 serving		300-375g (11-13oz)	Very hot oven 220°C, 425°F, Gas Mark 7 for 10-15 minutes
Wigeon	1 serving		675-900g (1½-2lb)	Very hot oven 220°C, 425°F, Gas Mark 7 for 15-25 minutes
GEESE	3-6 servings	As for duck	**Pink-footed** 1.8-3.1kg (4-7lb) **Greylag** 3.6-4.5kg (8-10lb) **Canada** 5.3-7.2kg (12-16lb)	Young goose – very hot oven 220°C, 425°F, Gas Mark 7, for 10 minutes then slow oven 170°C 325°F, Gas Mark 3 for 1 hour. Old goose – braise or stew
WOODPIGEON	1 serving	No close season	450-550g (1-1¼)	Very hot oven 220°C, 425°F, Gas Mark 7, for 20 minutes
HARES	6-8 servings	No close season but they may not be offered for sale from March –July inclusive	2.7-3.1kg (6-7lb)	Young hare – hot oven 200°C, 400°F, Gas Mark 6 for 20 minutes per 450g (1lb); slow oven 150°C, 300°F, Gas Mark 2 for 1½-2 hours
RABBITS	3 servings	No close season	1.1-1.5kg (2½-3½lb)	Hot oven 200°C, 400°F, Gas Mark 6 for 1 hour

TYPE OF GAME	Nº OF SERVINGS	SHOOTING SEASONS (DATES INCLUSIVE)	AVERAGE WEIGHT	APPROX. ROASTING TIMES/ TEMPERATURES
GROUSE	1-2 servings	August 12-December 10	550-675g (1¼-1½lb)	Moderately hot oven 190°C, 375°F Gas Mark 5 for 35 minutes
PTARMIGAN	1-2 servings	Scotland only, August 12-December 10	450-550g (1-1¼lb)	Roast (young birds) or braise
PARTRIDGE	1-2 servings	September 1-February 1	cock: 375-425g (13-15oz) hen: 365-415g (12½-14½oz)	Very hot oven 220°C, 425°F, Gas Mark 7 for 30 minutes
PHEASANT	3-4 servings	October 1-February 1	cock: 1.3-1.5kg (3-3½lb) hen: 900g-1.1kg (2-2½lb)	Moderately hot oven 190°C 375°F Gas Mark 5 for ¾-1 hour
COMMON SNIPE	1 serving (as a starter, 2 per person main course)	August 12-January 31	90-120g (3½- 4½oz)	Very hot oven 230°C, 450°F Gas Mark 8 for 6-15 minutes
WOODCOCK	1 serving	October 1-January 31 (England & Wales) September 1-January 31 (Scotland)	225-400g (8-14oz)	Very hot oven 220°C, 425°F Gas Mark 7 for 15-20 minutes

DEER	SEX	SHOOTING SEASON: ENGLAND		SCOTLAND
Roe	Buck Doe	April 1 - October 31 November 1 - February 28/29		April 1 - October 20 October 21 - March 31
Fallow	Buck Doe	August 1 - April 30 November 1 - February 28/29		July 1 - April 30 October 21- February 15
Red	Stag Hind	August 1 - April 30 November 1 - February 28/29		July 1 - October 20 October 21 - February 15

NOTES

Conversions are based on 25g=1oz, 570ml=1 pint and 2.5cm=1 inch. With larger amounts, quantities are rounded up or down. Do not mix metric and imperial measurements.

Ovens should be preheated to the specified temperature. Recipes can be adapted for Aga owners. Remember all ovens vary.

Onions – if button or pickling onions are not available, shallots can be substituted though they have a fuller flavour than onions. Alternatively a similar quantity of large onions, peeled, then quartered, sliced or chopped as appropriate, could be used as a substitute.

Vegetables – all vegetables should be cleaned and peeled, where appropriate, before use.

Fat – the use of fat is a matter of personal taste and butter or oil can, in most cases, be substituted for pork fat or dripping. Pork fat, useful for larding and barding game, is available from butchers.

Gamebirds – all recipes are for oven-ready birds.

Fish – all recipes, unless otherwise stated, are for cleaned fish.

Eggs – use size medium unless otherwise stated. Be careful using raw eggs especially if serving to young children, pregnant women or the elderly.

Stock – use home-made where possible. If using ready-made stock, a stock cube or tinned consommé, less salt may be required.

Crème fraîche can be substituted for cream in most recipes.

Redcurrant jelly – always use good quality redcurrant jelly in recipes as it dissolves more easily.

WHERE TO BUY GAME

Game can be bought from butchers and supermarkets as well as direct from a dealer.
To find your nearest game supplier, log on to:

www.gametoeat.co.uk

or contact:
The National Game Dealers Association,
18 Leaside, Aycliffe Industrial Park, Co Durham, DL5 6DE.
Tel: 01325 316320.
Fax: 01325 320634.
email: ngda@yorkshiregame.co.uk

Members of the National Game Dealers Association:

A&P Game
Cherrywood, Atbara Road, Church Crookham,
Hants GV13 OJ2.
Tel/fax: 01252 616599.
Contact: Mr Peter Fletcher.

Fayre Game Ltd, Unit 17, West Side Industrial Estate,
Jackson Street, St Helens, Merseyside WA9 3AT.
Tel: 01744 616120. Fax: 01744 616130.
Fax (London) 0207 635 4044.
Contact: Mr Chris Waters.

Gourmet Game, Park Cottage, Church End,
Frampton, Boston, Lincs PE20 1AH.
Tel: 01205 724274. Fax: 01205 722565.
Contact: Mr Crick Van Wyke.

Chris Jordan,
Beaumont House, Little Staughton, Beds MK44 2BH.
Tel/fax: 01234 376556.
Contact: Mr Chris Jordan.

Peterborough Game Company, Unit 7, The Arena,
Roman Bank, Bourne, Lincs PE10 9LQ.
Tel: 01788 393813. Fax: 01788 393800.
Contact: Mr Richard Bennett.

The National Game Dealers Association

Rick Bestwick Ltd,
Park Road, Holmewood Industrial Estate,
Chesterfield, Derbyshire S42 5UY.
Tel: 01246 854999. Fax: 01246 854968.
Contact: Mr Rick Bestwick.

Henry Stockdale,
Hill Farm, Mears Ashby, Northampton NN6 ODX.
Tel/fax: 01604 810206.
Contact: Mr Henry Stockdale.

Yorkshire Game Ltd,
18 Leaside, Aycliffe Industrial Park,
Newton Aycliffe, Co Durham DL5 6DE.
Tel: 01325 316320. Fax: 01325 320634.
Contact: Mrs Sandra Baxter.
Web address: www.yorkshiregame.co.uk

Allens, 117 Mount Street, Mayfair, London W1Y 6HX.
Tel: 0207 499 5831. Fax: 0207 409 7112.

Elveden Farms Ltd, Estate Office, Elveden,
Thetford, Norfolk IP24 3TQ.
Tel: 01842 890223. Fax: 01842 890070.
Contact: Mr J.W.Rudderham.

Hampshire Game, Pollards Farm, Clanville,
Andover, Hants SP11 9JE.
Tel: 01264 730294. Fax: 01264 730780.
Contact: Mr Steven Crouch.

Vicars Game, Reading Cold Store,
Deacon Way, Reading, Berkshire RG30 6AZ.
Tel/fax: 0118 945 5221.

For a list of dealers in Scotland, contact:

The Scottish Game Dealers Processors Association,
Kinloch Rannoch, by Pitlochry, Perthshire PH16 5QD.
Tel/fax: 01882 632260.
Contact: Mr Leo Barclay.

The National Game Dealers Association has been in existence for over 20 years. Its objects are to represent its members by the promotion of game production and consumption, and to secure adequate representation of the Association on all official bodies dealing with members' interests.

The **NGDA** is recognised by Government and is regularly consulted on industry matters. It works closely with all the main shooting organisations including The Game Conservancy Trust, the British Association for Shooting and Conservation and the Countryside Alliance.

The **NGDA** is currently working in partnership with the Countryside Alliance to promote the eating of game in the UK. Consumers should soon begin to see information in game outlets on the nutritional value of game, with cooking tips and recipes.

The cottage industry image of game has long gone. It is now processed in modern, fully-equipped and controlled factories which conform to the standards demanded by the British Meat Industry. If the local butcher still processes his own game, he must do so following a strict hygiene code.

The British public can buy game with confidence and is doing so. British game is enjoying a rebirth. Forget the myth. Modern game producers do *not* hang the birds until the meat has a strong, potent flavour. Such is its versatility that it can be cooked in both traditional and modern ways – roasted with seasonal fruits, casseroled, barbecued or even stir-fried.

Sandra Baxter
Chairman, National Game Dealers Association

CONVERSION TABLES

OVEN TEMPERATURES

	ELECTRICITY		GAS MARK
	Degrees Centigrade	Degrees Fahrenheit	
Very cool	110	225	¼
	120	250	½
Cool	140	275	1
	150	300	2
Moderate	160	325	3
	180	350	4
Moderately hot	190	375	5
Hot	200	400	6
	220	425	7
Very hot	230	450	8

LIQUID MEASURES

4fl oz = 100ml	2 pints = 1.2 litres
¼ pint (5fl oz) = 150ml	2¼ pints = 1.3 litres
8fl oz = 250ml	2½ pints = 1.5 litres
½ pint (10fl oz) = 275ml	2¾ pints = 1.6 litres
¾ pint (15fl oz) = 450ml	3 pints = 1.75 litres
1 pint (20fl oz) = 570ml	3½ pints = 2 litres
1¼ pints = 750ml	4 pints = 2.25 litres
1½ pints = 900ml	4½ pints = 2.5 litres
1¾ pints = 1 litre	5 pints = 2.75 litres

LENGTH

⅛in = 3mm	
¼in = 5mm	
½in = 1cm	
¾in = 2cm	
1in = 2.5cm	
1½in = 4cm	
2in = 5cm	
2½in = 6cm	
3in = 7.5cm	
3½in = 9cm	
4in = 10cm	
5in = 12.5cm	
6in = 15cm	
7in = 18cm	
8in = 20cm	
9in = 23cm	
10in = 25cm	
11in = 28cm	
12in = 30cm	

SOLID MEASURES

¼ oz = 10g	12oz = 350g
½ oz = 15g	13oz = 375g
¾ = 20g	14oz = 400g
1oz = 25g	15oz = 425g
1½ = 40g	1lb = 450g
2oz = 50g	1¼ lb = 550g
2½oz = 65g	1½ lb = 675g
3oz = 75g	1¾ lb = 800g
3½oz = 90g	2lb = 900g
4oz = 100g	2¼ lb = 1kg
4½oz = 120g	2½ lb = 1.1kg
5oz = 150g	3lb = 1.3kg
5½oz = 165g	3½ lb = 1.5kg
6oz = 175g	4lb = 1.8kg
6½oz = 185g	4½ lb = 2kg
7oz = 200g	5lb = 2.3kg
7½oz = 215g	6lb = 2.7kg
8oz = 225g	7lb = 3.1kg
9oz = 250g	8lb = 3.6kg
10oz = 275g	9lb = 4kg
11oz = 300g	10lb = 4.5kg

index